TWENTY
STEPS
TO
POWER,

INFLUENCE AND CONTROL
OVER PEOPLE

by

H. W. GABRIEL

PRENTICE-HALL, INC., ENGLEWOOD CLIFFS
NEW JERSEY

Forty-first Printing . . . . . August 1987

PRINTED IN THE UNITED STATES OF AMERICA

93497—B&P

TO THE DESERVING FEW WHO
WILL WELL USE THE POWER
THEY ARE ABOUT TO ACQUIRE

PREFACE

Real personal power, self power, is undoubtedly the most sought for of all the wants of people everywhere. Like you, all people see it as a road to anything that is a desire. Some seek and find it, some find it and lose it, and some never find it. And some of these last become so obsessed with a desire for it that the futile seeking of it drives them to madness.

Everyone who seeks self power searches not only for its secrets but also for a simplified and practical means for achieving it quickly and surely. All of this has at last been packaged for you. The secrets of self power are in the *Twenty Steps to Power, Influence and Control Over People,* and those twenty steps are the simplified and practical techniques, the techniques that the successes of centuries have developed.

Everyone has an appetite for real and genuine self power, and you are one of them. Some merely wish for it hopefully but indifferently. Some crave it with an unreasonableness (and lack of aptitude) that is not unlike the unreasonable cravings of pregnancy. And some hunger for it ambitiously,—drivingly and consumingly,—seeing in it the means to prestige, security, dominance and all the other things that ambition aims toward.

No matter which of these you might be, no matter how little or much of self power you want, the *Twenty Steps to Power, Influence and Control Over People* will contribute toward a fuller and more satisfying life for you. They are twenty steps you and everyone should at least climb part way. And if you are among those who hunger ambitiously for self power, they are twenty steps that take you there faster than any elevator or escalator you have dreamed of.

v

You who have had to stand aside while less meek and less worthy persons acquired power and passed you by no longer need to stifle your ambitions. Self power, influence and control are as much a potential in you as in anyone, and no one had more of either to start with,—but somewhere those others found their want of them and got the "feel" for them. Now you can too.

Self power and its rewards are not things that one must strive for laboriously, as the *Twenty Steps to Power, Influence and Control Over People* quickly proves. You can take your time, leisurely and cautiously traveling step by step, or you can leap along in strides that carry you two or three steps at a time onward. Whether you travel unhurriedly or hurriedly, the twenty steps are both your quickest and your surest means to self power achievement. Despite this, they are here so simplified for you that they deprive you of all excuses you may ever have had for not going on toward success.

The *Twenty Steps to Power, Influence and Control Over People* is a book you will read and live with and reread. In spite of yourself, it will lift you somewhere whether you have purpose or not.

TABLE OF CONTENTS

vii

1

RECOGNIZE THE SECRETS OF REAL PERSONAL POWER

There are four secrets of success of real personal power.

Real personal power strikes instantly.

Real personal power makes others want to bend to you.

Real personal power makes others want to perform for you.

Real personal power makes others want to enjoy a bond with you.

"That man *has* something."

You say it,—you *feel* it,—and even though you don't put a tag on it you're lifted up by it and wish you had it too.

1. Tag it and recognize it for what it is

When you said, "That man *has* something," you reacted to him the way *he* wanted *you* to react. *He hit you with his personal power!*

Right there is the first big secret of real personal power. *It strikes instantly.*

When you have real personal power it is seen and felt the instant anyone gets his first glimpse of you. That is the personal power you want. Maybe you already have some one of the

1

other kinds, the kinds that come from your "growing on people," or from their recognition of your capabilities or accomplishments, but those are too slow. They can bring you at best a *limited* personal power and bring it eventually, but you want a full and effective personal power and you want it now!

And you are going to have it. The tricks and techniques of it will soon be yours and then your personal power will smite others as instantly as any has ever smitten you.

2. Others must bend to you

You are fed up with all the hog-wash about the "good fellow" approach. You are anxious to get along with people but you want them to be anxious to get along with you too. You have had your fill of all the platitudes on bending to the other fellow in order to win him,—you want him to bend to you!

And that's what he is going to do.

Repeat it to yourself, you want him to bend to you. And tell yourself, that's what he is going to do.

Now tell yourself why he is going to bend to you. Tell yourself he'll do so because you are going to make him do so. More important,—you are going to make him do so voluntarily and willingly! In other words, you are going to make him *want* to bend to you.

Now you have hit on the second big secret of real personal power. *It makes others want to bend to you.*

3. Others must perform for you

When you have real personal power it pulls others,—it draws them to you, makes them want to know you, and makes them want to please you. That is the personal power you want.

Maybe you already have some one of the other kinds, the kinds where your authority over people, or else a club you threaten them with, makes them bend to you and do your bidding, but those kinds are too precarious. They can bring you a *doubtful* personal power that exists whenever you brandish them, but you want a positive personal power, one that does not require brandishing authority or other clubs and is ever and always effective.

You are tired of all the poppycock about magic words that win people over to you. You want people to try to win you over to them. You are disgusted with all the so-touted tricks for getting people's cooperation or customers' orders,—you want people to offer and press these on you!

And that's what they are going to do.

Repeat it to yourself, you want them to press their cooperation on you. And tell yourself, that's what they are going to do.

Now tell yourself why they will do it. Tell yourself they'll do it because you are going to make them want to do so. And biggest of all,—they are going to want to do so because they want to perform for you!

Now you have hit on the third big secret of real personal power. *It makes others want to perform for you.*

4. Others must want a bond with you

When you have real personal power it hypnotizes others,—it makes them center on you, makes them feel something of themselves is attached to you, and makes them enjoyably feel you as important to them. That is the personal power you want.

You are bored with all the tomfoolery about putting yourself on a common ground with others. You want others to strive for footing on what is your own ground. And you are weary of all the nonsense about needing to establish a bond with others,— you want them to try to establish a bond with you!

And that's what they are going to do.

Repeat it to yourself, you want them to try to establish a bond with you. And tell yourself, that's what they are going to do.

Now again tell yourself why they will. Tell yourself they'll try because you are going to make them want a bond with you. And most to the point,—they are going to want a bond with you because your importance to them will create the desire for it!

Now you have hit on the fourth big secret of real personal power. *It makes others want to enjoy a bond with you.*

5. A small price buys it all

Whenever you have a personal power that does all four of those, you have the real personal power. Whenever a personal power fails to do any of those it is not a real personal power, it is only a partial one or a false one. But you don't want a partial one or a false one,—you've had enough of that sort of thing,—you want real personal power. The question now is, what is it going to cost you?

Strangely, whereas false and partial personal power may cost you all manner of things, *real* personal power costs you only one thing,—the sacrifice and abandonment of some of your indolence.

And for that small price, what does it give you? It makes others instantly conscious of you and your power; it makes others bend to you; it makes others want to perform for you; and it makes others want to enjoy a bond with you. With all of that, what more could you want? But you do want one thing more,—you want the thing that made you want real personal power in the first place,—you want the benefits that can be derived from those!

6. Others will make your way theirs

Right here and now, let's not kid each other and you quit kidding yourself. You're not seeking popularity nor any "he's a jolly good fellow" award. You're seeking personal power,—the real thing. Bending to the other guy and meeting him on common ground can make you a "good fellow," but being a "good fellow" can never bring you real personal power. Magic words and hypocritical fawning can win others to accept or like you and make you popular, but popularity can never bring you real personal power. You know, because you've tried those things!

When you have real personal power, everyone will be a good fellow toward you,—and they'll court popularity with you. When you have real personal power you don't have to go their way,—they'll come your way! And that's what you want.

Whether you're an industrialist, a politician, a supervisor, a salesman, a banker, a clergyman, or what you are, you will always measure your personal power by how much others come your way.

7. The most important time period in your life

So much for that. Now, without kidding yourself, and answering honestly, how much have you got of what it takes? If you aren't sure, go find a full-length mirror and size up the man you see there.

Take a good look at him. Does he instantly arrest your attention? Does he have a distinctiveness that would make him stand out singly in any crowd? Does his distinctiveness compel your eyes to stay on him? Is there something about him that makes you want to know him? Does it pull you toward him, make you feel you'd like to please him? Remember, since he is only an image, he has to do all this without uttering a word!

Does he?

If he does, then you can jump along the first few steps rather rapidly, just picking up from them some refreshers. But if he doesn't, comb through the next few chapters carefully, for in that case they are for you the most important steps in your climb. They cover the all-important first sixty seconds of impression creation that exists each time anyone sees you. Day in and day out, that sixty seconds is over and over again the most important time period in your life. Without complete success every one of the hundreds or thousands of times per day that that time period occurs, real personal power is not possible to you.

8. "Getting along with others" never means power over them

Remind yourself once again of the first secret of real personal power: It strikes instantly!

You must concentrate on that one factor of real personal power first for, until you have mastered this first secret of real personal power, all the so-called "things to say" and "how to say them," important though they are, are meaningless,—are nothing more than hints on "how to get along with people."

Those things alone can never bring you real personal power, —at most, they can only bring you a little wider acceptance and a little more of pleasant relationships. If you haven't already found that out for yourself, ask every man who has ever tried them. No matter how many authors or lecturers try to sell them as "keys" to personal power, they never are keys to personal power. There is a vast difference between "getting along with others" and having a personal power over others.

Getting along with others is important. In fact, you must be able to get along with others before you can make them want to get along with you. In other words, the ability to get along with others is a prerequisite to acquiring real personal power over them. It is a prerequisite to real personal power just as much as vocal cords are to oratory,—it is essential, but it in itself never leads to or gives you that personal power, just as vocal cords in themselves never lead to or make you an orator.

9. Words are better as a tool than as a power

If your personal power is to strike instantly, your personal power must be visible,—instantly visible. Therefor, your personal power cannot be dependent on what you say or how you say it,—for anything that is dependent for success on what you say and how you say it is not visible.

Thus again, if you *now* do not instantly arrest attention,—if you now do not have a distinctiveness that makes you stand out singly in a crowd,—if you now do not have a distinctiveness that compels eyes to stay on you,—if you now do not have a distinctiveness that pulls others toward you and makes them want to please you, these next few chapters are the most important reading you have ever done.

Heretofore you have put your first reliance on what you said and how you said it (whether you were selling, supervising, lecturing, or whatever). Those things are still important, but from here on you must learn to quit relying on them *as* a personal power and begin to use them as *tools* of your personal power.

10. The first secret must be mastered first

You are seeking *real* personal power. You know the four secrets of it,—you recognize them,—you have observed they are the secret of the power of everyone you have ever seen who has real personal power. What you are after now is to bring those secrets to yourself,—to make them work for you.

To a limited extent, you can accomplish the second, third and fourth of those secrets in several ways. However, don't try to jump the gun on them! There is only one way you can accomplish them fully, and that is by mastering the first secret of real personal power first.

11. Begin now to put visible power together piece by piece

At this point, almost every seeker of personal power begins to get cold feet. If you are like most of them, you can easily visualize yourself as accomplishing the second, third and fourth secrets of personal power but you have doubts as to whether you can master the first secret. To put it bluntly, you are doubting whether you can make yourself into a striking personality!

Many others have done it. Face up to the facts the way they did. Can you master that first secret of real personal power? Of course you can! Remind yourself here and now, no matter who or what you are, you are far better equipped to do so than many of the most famous people who have.

Take a look at a few on the list. An exiled little weakling of only four feet ten did it and became the greatest man in the history of Rome. A cripple did it and became the most powerful political figure of the world. A ridiculous looking, uneducated, clownish nobody did it and became so powerful it took all the might of the modern world to stop him. The list of such examples runs into the hundreds! And they too, like you, at first had doubts and made mistakes. But, once they recognized the four secrets of real personal power and that the whole key to it rests in mastering the first secret first, they went on to heights that all lesser men only dream about.

You can master that first secret of real personal power, but you must put it together piece by piece. Its pieces are the first steps of the climb to real personal power, and they begin with your determining what personal power will mean to you and just what kind of personal power you want. *Now*, not tomorrow, is the time to begin.

12. Points worth special attention

1. Real personal power costs only the abandonment of some unwanted indolence.

2. Your personal power must be visible, not reliant on what you say.

3. How much others come your way is the measure of what real personal power you have.

4. The whole key to real personal power rests in mastering its first secret first.

5. You are far better equipped to master real personal power than many of the famous people who have.

2

HOW TO EVALUATE PERSONAL POWER
AND ITS USES

> Real personal power is the means for dealing with people successfully.
>
> Courting others blocks the paths to real personal power.
>
> False personal power is only agency power, dependent on ladder status, rein control or club possession.
>
> Real personal power is the power of self alone to affect others, and thus is self power.

If you are going to build yourself into a person of real personal power, you first of all need something to build on and something to build toward. It's much the same as building a house; you need the ground, properly prepared, and need a blueprint (or at least a visual picture) of what the finished product is to consist of and be.

1. Why you are interested in being a personal power

Since you are interested in building yourself into a person of real personal power, you're interested in dealing with people. You must be, for personal power, real or false, never exists as a power except when it is exercised on people.

9

Here again, let's not kid each other. You have selfish reasons for wanting personal power. If you didn't, it wouldn't be important enough to you for you to be troubling to build it.

Let's add up that much of it: You are interested in building yourself into a personal power because you have selfish reasons for wanting to exercise it on the people you deal with.

Admitting that much to yourself forces you to admit one more thing: Success in dealing with others is for personal selfish reasons exceedingly important to you.

Don't be ashamed to admit it. Come right out loud and say it! Again, if it weren't true, you wouldn't be troubling to build yourself into a personal power. And only by admitting it, at least to yourself, will you be able to be a real personal power.

2. "Get along" with others as you deal with them

When you have admitted that success in dealing with others is for personal selfish reasons exceedingly important to you and is why you are interested in being a personal power, you come face to face with one more fact: You recognize your objective (that personal selfish reason) as being dependent on your success in dealing with others. (Objectives that *aren't* have no need of personal power.)

With that being the case, if you are going to build yourself into a personal power you must build on your dealing with others. To do this, you must first prepare the ground; that is, make your present dealing with others be such as you can build on.

This means one thing: In dealing with others, you must "get along" with them.

Maybe you already do. If so, so much the better. You have a head start. Nevertheless, it will still be to your advantage to check on yourself.

3. Pull in your horns and ignore those of others

You will always need to get along with people. Later, as you build into a real personal power, the problem will lessen because people then will be interested in getting along with you. In the meantime, however, the burden rests on you,—you need to get along with them regardless of whether they are interested in getting along with you.

Because you are building yourself into a power, and because the twenty steps that make you one consist of techniques for dealing with people in a manner that will make them want to get along with you, only two rules are important at this point in your getting along with others.

One: Pull in your horns a bit. Take the emphasis off aggressiveness and put it on cooperative pleasantness (*not* affected congeniality however). Cease acting and speaking authoritatively and instead let your manner and words bespeak and call for mutual interest and cooperation. And particularly, be less anxious to do the talking and more willing to do some listening!

Two: Ignore other people's horns. Don't let the rudeness, discourtesy and inconsiderateness of others irritate you (or at least don't let your irritation show or be heard). Don't let others pull you into an argument (no matter how unright they are). Most of all (and except for actual wrongs), make it a point "not to see or hear" anything you disapprove of!

4. Prepare for attracting others by abandoning courting of them

At the same time that you are pulling in your horns and ignoring those of others, you should be abandoning many of your previous habits of getting along with people. Remember, you are preparing to build yourself into a personal power.

As you well know, in ordinary circumstances (i.e., when you are not building yourself into a personal power), the courting of others (using flattery, solicitousness, deference, etc. on them) is a common means of getting along with them. Discontinue it immediately! You are going to be causing *them* to want to court you and you cannot do it if you are courting them.

Discontinuing the courting of others does not mean abandoning warmth and friendliness toward others. It does not mean refraining from giving others deserved compliments. And it does not mean nonaccordance of respect due others. To the contrary, it means genuinizing these things by divesting them of all liegemanship and toadying extras.

Any ingratiating tactics taint you with obsequiousness and cause others to regard themselves as important to you instead of regarding you as important to them. Be mindful always of the fourth secret of real personal power. Instead of showing yourself as seeking a bond with others you must create in them a desire to seek a bond with you.

This is as applicable in management, sales, finance, and everywhere else, as it is in politics, but the most dramatic examples are supplied by the top personal power personalities of World War Two. Mussolini, after years of building himself into a personal power, surrendered his strength when he courted Hitler instead of causing Hitler to court him. Stalin surrendered his in turn likewise to Hitler. Then Roosevelt surrendered his by courting Stalin instead of making Stalin court him. The successors of Stalin, having learned their lesson from his courting of Hitler, have ever since refused to court anyone. Meanwhile Tito, refusing to court anyone, has managed to remain a secure personal power "island" that none dare to court because of the foreknowledge that to do so would make him the greatest personal power of all!

The same things happen between industries (especially in merger pictures) and between individuals at all levels of the power ladder. In any analysis, your being a real personal power always is finally dependent on your ability to create in others the desire to seek a bond with you. The further steps that follow will show you how,—but you must prepare for them by starting *your* non-courting now. (Women have known the basic tricks of it for ages!)

5. You are going to know what, why and how

As you carefully avoid courting others and focus your attention on your two revised rules for getting along with people, you also need to prepare the ground in other ways. Mostly, you need to take a realistic view of personal power itself.

Too often you have looked on the real personal power with awe. You have imagined it as a complex, massive, God-given force that is bestowed on only a chosen few. But it isn't. It's just the opposite. Despite its strength, it's a remarkably simple, concentrated, acquired force that is achievable to anyone (who has sufficient purpose and gumption to go after it).

Since you are going to go after this real personal power, and going to try to hold on to it when you get it, you must always have your eyes wide open to that truth. If you ever close your eyes to it and start looking upon yourself as someone "favored by the gods," some other with his eyes open will sweep away your personal power and make you a has-been!

To strengthen yourself, know a little about personal power. Know who wants it and why. And most of all, know why *you* want it.

People have wanted personal power ever since the second man came into existence. Some have achieved it, most never have and never will, but those who do achieve it do so because they have the courage to look it straight in the face and see it as what it is. And that's what you must do.

If you truly want real personal power you can acquire it. And the techniques set forth here for you will make it simple to do so. But they make it simple for you only because they also give you a thorough understanding of its factors. Unless you gather in and absorb every crumb of that understanding before using any of the techniques, the techniques can boomerang.

Every year thousands of persons strive toward personal power,—and most of them fail. So that you won't be one of those who fail, you are going to know what personal power is, why it is, and how and what makes it be.

6. Both false and real power can be misused

You can speak of personal power loftily, idealistically, and so on, but you still must recognize that you (as everyone else) are interested in it primarily (if not solely) for selfish reasons. Personal power, whether real or false, isn't an instrument reserved to the scrupulous or honorable or sincere. It could make the world utopian if it were, and it is hoped you are one of these, but personal power is as equally in the reach of the unscrupulous as it is yours.

And you must give recognition to a further fact: In all cases, wherever real personal power exists, it itself is the same; the same secrets make it work, and the same elements constitute it. The only differences that ever exist with it are the ways in which and purposes for which it is used.

Reflect a moment on how some of your acquaintances wield "tiny bits" of false personal power. There's Joe Goof, for example (every group of acquaintances has a Joe Goof in it). When you go to lunch with him he delights in making a false display of "importance"—he likes to keep waitresses hopping just for the satisfaction of doing it.

And of course every group has a Jim Whoozit in it also. He makes use of one of the oldest of all tricks of false personal power gathering. Because of that "inside track" he has (or pretends to have) to the "people who count," he has everyone being "carefully nice" to him.

When you see what gloating satisfaction millions of these "little" persons get from misusing all manner of small and false personal power, how can you be surprised or horrified that other persons (or you) will misuse big and real personal power? How sure are you that you won't be one of them?

7. False personal power is agency power

Here and now, let's nail down the difference between false personal power and the real personal power, self power. You encounter both constantly (thousands more of the false than the real) and both, of necessity, are referred to time and time again in these pages, so a clean cut distinction between them is necessary.

First of all, false personal power is not personal power. Instead, it is agency power, power that a person has solely (a) because of ladder status (social, political, executive, etc.), (b) because of rein control (financial, supply, matrimonial, etc.) or (c) because of club possession (authority, violence, exposure, etc.). In other words, though the person is the agent of the power and the power is exercised by the person, the power does not come from the person; it comes from his or her club, reins or ladder rung.

When you defer to such a person you do so, not because you are *attracted* to him or her, but because to not defer to him or her might cost you in some manner. Let him or her be deprived of the club, reins or ladder rung and you would not defer and might even either despise or ignore him or her as a nonentity.

Thus, false personal power is not a visible power. Sight of the person does not show his or her power. His or her power is unseen and is not known until his or her club, reins or ladder rung are made known to you. Even then, he or she is still not a power if the particular club, reins or ladder rung do not in some manner affect you (unless you're an idolizer).

8. The only real personal power is self power

Now let's take a look at real personal power. First of all, real personal power is visible. Everyone sees it and it strikes instantly, long before anyone knows whether you have any club, reins or ladder rung.

Next, when you have real personal power people defer to you because they are attracted to you and not because failure to do so might cost them. It is *you*, not your club, reins or ladder rung, that they defer to.

Thus, the power is emanated by you. Plainly, *you* (not a club, reins or ladder rung) are the power.

Because such a power is so different from false personal power—because it is visible, strikes instantly, attracts others, causes them to bend toward you, causes them to perform for you, causes them to seek a bond with you, causes them to come your way, and comes from your self alone—it needs a name all its own that can prevent it from ever being thought of or confused with agency power (the false personal power). For this reason, real personal power, the power of self alone to affect others, is hereafter referred to as self power.

9. Appraise your power performance beforehand

Despite the vast difference there is between self power and agency power, one of the best ways to get a picture of what you will do with self power is to appraise what you have done with such agency power as you have had from time to time. Make the appraisal now, and make it often in the future. Frankly, it will be ten times harder to change to an idealist after you develop personal power than it will be now so, if you want to be one (and I and the whole world hope you do), make your determining appraisal at once so you can modify yourself into that idealist *now*.

Recently a personal power experiment was tried with eight men and three women. The latter consisted of a business-woman, a professional woman, and a homebody. The men were equally diversified and ranged from an electrician to a college professor. Except for general popularity and some modest agency power, all of the men and women were entirely devoid of personal power, and none knew they were participating in an experiment.

One by óne, each of the eleven was appointed to a "prestige" post in public organizations. Each post, however, opened the opportunity for the wielding of extensive personal power (agency power). Two of the eleven (a broker and the home-body) quickly tired of having pressure put upon them to use their "personal power" to benefit this person and that and so they resigned. Three others (a salesman, a wholesale merchant, and the professional woman) took their assignments seriously, regarded their obligations gravely, and in general refused to be pressured into any serious misuse of their newly gained power.

The remaining six were overwhelmed by and greedily joy-ous of the new "personal" power that was theirs to wield. Four of them used it (in different ways) as dishonestly as does any racketeer. A fifth used it for fraudulent manipulations. The sixth used it both vengefully and to trade for valuable favors.

The experiment is mentioned here for one reason only: To help you appraise your own power performance. You are just as human as those eleven persons and the chances are that one of them (insofar as use of power) is your counterpart. None was a pure idealist, as you can see. Two were puritan but not idealists. Three were idealists but not puritans. And the re-mainder were neither, but instead were opportunists.

10. Points worth special attention

1. You are interested in dealing with people.
2. You are interested in building yourself into a real personal power be-cause you have selfish reasons for wanting to exercise it on the people you deal with.
3. To be successful in dealing with others, you must first "get along" with them.
4. Pull in your horns a bit.
5. Ignore the horns of others.
6. Never court others.
7. Aim toward attracting others.
8. It is self power, not agency power, that attracts others to you.
9. Make a power performance appraisal of yourself now, and make them often in the future.

3

HOW TO START YOUR OWN POWER GENERATING

The five key factors in proper human intercourse are proper
courtesy, respect, deference, politeness and manners.

These key factors, when wholly devoid of submissiveness,
are the foundation stones of eminence and self power.

Diligent adherence to the concepts of the foundation stones
initiates the leveler technique.

The leveler technique makes people more aware of you
and causes them to grant you a higher level.

Putting the full leveler technique into operation gives you
a power feel and starts your self power generating.

Until now, you have had little or no awareness of how
much of liegemanship there was in your ordinary habits of getting along with people. Discontinuing the courting of others
wipes away some of it, and ignoring their horns wipes away a lot
more, but there are still stronger habits of liegemanship you
must wipe away also.

1. Properness never requires submissiveness

From childhood on, certain things in your relations with
people and your getting along with them have been confused

18

for you. These have all centered on improper confusions of courtesy, respect, deference, politeness and manners, and have resulted from submissiveness being emphasized as a necessary characteristic of each. (Which it isn't!)

Before going on toward your removal of submissiveness as a characteristic of these relations with others, let's examine each individually and pinpoint exactly what it calls for from you. All of them are essential in your getting along with others but submissiveness cannot be a characteristic as you use any of them if you are to build yourself into a self power.

2. The foundation stones of eminence and self power

(a) If you are to get along with people and at the same time attract them to you, courtesy toward them is a must. However, courtesy does not call upon you to figuratively, in words or manner, bow or curtsy to them. It means only that you accord them graceful and tactful considerateness; that you *be* considerate of them willingly and kindly, not duteously or grumpily. (Reply promptly when addressed, acknowledge their rights and feelings, etc.)

(b) To get along with others and at the same time attract them to you also requires respect toward them. Respect, however, does not call upon you to elevate or station them above you. It means only that you acknowledge and consider them; that you be cognizant of them and of whatever individuality they possess. (Honor them as people, honor their individuality, their accomplishments, their office, etc.)

(c) Similarly, getting along with others and attracting them to you requires deference toward them. Deference, though, does not call upon you to yield or submit to them. It means only that you show a regard for their opinions, knowledge, authority, abilities, and the like; that you give notice to these and make due and proper allowance for the other having them. (For example: If a man has been assigned to direct traffic, follow his direction; if a plumber has been called in, and you aren't one, don't try to tell him how to do his job; etc.)

(d) In getting along with others and attracting them to you, politeness too is essential. Here likewise, politeness does not call upon you to be servile toward another. It means only that you practice (by word and action) a cultured regard for the status, actions, customs and beliefs of a person consistent with the place and occasion; that you *do* what good breeding calls for in the circumstance. (Thank persons for a courtesy or service, even when it is their job to provide it; help another with his or her coat; let another finish before speaking; leave your shoes at the doorstep of the household where such is the custom; etc.)

(e) Getting along with others and attracting them to you also demands manners of you. Again though, manners do not call upon you to bow to people, give way to them, or even to accord them acceptance. Manners mean only that you deport yourself in a self-respectful way and that it be such as will not be offensive, rude or censurable by those transacting with you, encountering you, in the vicinity of you, or in company with you; that, mainly, your deportment is governed by propriety and never guilty of lack of considerateness for others. (Don't embarrass even the lowliest person by bawling him or her out publicly; don't make a spectacle of yourself eating, drinking, dancing or otherwise; don't shove ahead of persons who are properly waiting their turn; don't introduce topics that will offend or embarrass others; etc.)

These recounted concepts of the five key factors in proper human intercourse can well be called the foundation stones of eminence and self power. How much they will be so for you depends on how completely you make them devoid of submissiveness.

3. Never consign yourself to a lesser level

In setting forth those foundation stones here they are set forth as concepts that need thorough acceptance and diligent adherence preliminary to engaging in the practice of the first of your self power techniques, the leveler technique.

Emphasis must be put on the fact that submissiveness has no place in true and proper courtesy, respect, deference, politeness and manners. When submissiveness becomes a part of any of them, they no longer are true and proper but are instead reduced to duteous or servile practices. When this is the case, no matter what title you carry, others see you, not on their plane, but on a plane of lesser level.

Your objective, at this point, is to have others regard you as on *their* plane (*or higher*), no matter what title they carry.

4. Put greater emphasis on exercise of the five stones

When you were a child, the five foundation stones, to one extent or another, were taught you. At the same time, quite unfortunately, you were also taught submissiveness. It is not unfortunate that you were taught submissiveness,—what is unfortunate is that you were taught it concurrently.

In teaching you submissiveness, your elders taught you to give way to elders, to yield to their superiority (in age, knowledge, authority), to accept and follow their dictates, and to answer with a "Yes, sir" or "No, sir" when spoken to. As a liege of your parents, this and other submissiveness was due them from you. Similarly, the same submissiveness is due anyone of whom you might be a liege today (if you are one), but not any other.

Because submissiveness was taught to you concurrently with the five foundation stones, you regarded it as a part of them. You came to regard giving way to others as synonymous with courtesy, manners and politeness. You came to look upon yielding to others as synonymous with respect and deference. And so on. But the five foundation stones have at last made a proper distinction for you.

With the distinction made, your job now is to effect the separation. If you are a liege (and very few people aren't) submissiveness from you is still a due of someone. Despite this, and even while according that submissiveness, eliminate submissiveness from the courtesy, respect, deference, politeness and manners you exercise and give these stones greater attention than you ever have before. Your elimination of submissiveness from these things is essential and is the first factor of the leveler technique.

5. The core of the leveler technique

Submissiveness is just one of three factors that cause others to see you on a plane that is of lesser level. You can eliminate it as a factor with all persons except the one or two to whom it may be due, but you can eliminate the other factors even with these persons. As a consequence, and despite the fact that you must continue submissiveness toward an employer or some other benefactor, you can cause even these persons to elevate the level of their regard of you.

The second factor in the leveler technique is the elimination of "No, sir" and "Yes, sir," and all other uses of sir and ma'am, from your vocabulary.

Henceforth, always use the person's name or title. In addition, in all instances where you heretofore have used a simple "Yes, sir" or "No, sir," use a brief sentence. For example, a question might be put to you as, "Have you been to lunch yet?" Don't reply, "No, sir" nor "No, Mr. Pennyweight"; instead say, "No, Mr. Pennyweight, I haven't."

If the person addressed has a title, simply use his title. Such as, "No, Professor, I haven't." Or, "No, Doctor, I haven't." Or even, "No, Colonel, I haven't."

Remember, use a brief sentence, not just the person's name or title. There is an important reason for this. Often, when only the name or title is used, it sounds flippant or curt. When a brief sentence is used (the more brief, the better) this cannot happen—unless you cause it intentionally.

These things may seem small and unimportant, but they are

very much the opposite. The change they effect in your own attitude is tremendous and the other results are equally remarkable. Try them for twenty-four hours and be convinced.

The elimination of sir and the substitution of names and titles accomplishes three basic things for you simultaneously. (a) It instantly releases you from a symbolism of subjugation and thus erases "difference of level" from your mind, which was there whether you were conscious of it or not. (b) It deprives the other of any acknowledgement from you of "difference of level" and compels him to either accept that there is none or make himself ridiculous by trying to impose some other barrier. (c) It shows observers you do not acknowledge a "difference of level" with any individual.

Following immediately on those three basic accomplishments, the elimination of sir accomplishes a fourth thing that is exceedingly important to your building of self power: It instantly makes all people much more aware of you; and you more aware of your individuality.

This fourth accomplishment can well be said to be the *reason* for the elimination of sir (and its equivalents). And when we regard it in this manner we see the first three as explanations of how this fourth is brought about.

Most definitely, you will feel people as more aware of you at once. When a customer asks if you can ship before the end of the month, instead of saying "Yes, sir" say, "Yes, Mr. Abernathy, I can." And when the chief executive of your company bellows and asks if you are an idiot, instead of saying "No, sir" say, "No, Mr. Fitzgerald, I'm not." In these and all cases, people will have a greater awareness of you and you'll begin to benefit from the change immediately.

Ask any man who has built himself into a self power; he'll tell you he got his first feel of individuality and self power *and of his power generating* when he first did what you are doing. This core of the leveler technique is your first actual "power" tool so put it to work at once.

6. The third factor in the leveler technique

The third factor in the leveler technique is just as important and easy as the first two but, like everyone else, you'll be more reluctant to use it. Nevertheless, you must!

At this point, remind yourself of two things: The purpose of the leveler technique is not to "cut anyone down to size" or reduce their level. To the contrary, its purpose is to enable you to get along better with people while you at the same time make them more aware of you and make them grant you a higher level (no matter *how high* your level already is).

If you are an organization man or a salesman, the chances are you are on a mutual first name basis with the executive above you, those just below you, and all the persons closely associated with you. They all call you George (or whatever your name is) and you call them Tom, Dick, Harry, Ethel, Mary, Bob, Jim, Joe and so on. Now, and without becoming a stuffed shirt, you're going to change all that.

You aren't concerned here with whether or not "familiarity breeds contempt." The fact you are concerned with is that familiarity is shortsighted. And it's tenacious.

The name George was used for you above for a special reason. It's the name of a young and very competent man who became president of a company when his father died unexpectedly. Until that day, everyone, from the other directors down to the janitors, had known him has Georgie. And Georgie he remained.

He was brilliant and (as later events proved) even more competent than his father. Nevertheless, and despite his title, everyone saw him only as Georgie and as a consequence refused to take him or his orders very seriously.

Less competent men would have let time take care of the situation. Less rational men would have made wholesale replacements in the organization. George, however, faced up to the problem squarely.

Your situation probably isn't the same as George's was,— but your problem is the same. You must make people raise their level of regard for you. Instead of seeing you nose to nose, they must see you from a few feet away so as to see you more as an individual and less as but one of the organization.

The same applies to the customers you sell, the tradespeople you buy from, and everyone else. But, begin the change *now*, and make it quickest with those you work amongst.

As your first move toward having others abandon use of your first name, cease to use first names in addressing or referring to the executives above you. At the same time, cease using first names in addressing your secretary and any other of the females in your organization. The reactions will vary but, if you use miss and mister in as natural a manner as you used their first names, the reactions won't be unfavorable and will be short lived regardless.

As your second move, cease using first names in addressing or referring to associates, customers, and the equivalents. Some of your associates will bristle or treat it as a joke the first day or two but, if you persist with it in a natural manner and without explaining or arguing it, they'll soon accept it.

Instances can occur where your associates demand an explanation, but with rare exceptions these occur only because *you* have not handled the 'mister' in a natural manner or because *you* have let it also produce some change in your relationship with them.

When such an instance occurs, with one of your associates trying to "pin you down" on the abandonment of his first name by saying something such as, "Why are you giving me this 'mister' business?" don't explain or argue, merely comment, "I think you deserve a mister." If he uses a why or another question to press the point, a safe comment is, "I think your being 'mistered' will emphasize and help your business status." And if he presses further with, "And I suppose you want me to 'mister' you!" comment, "Only if you feel I deserve it."

The same procedure should be used if your secretary or anyone else tries to press for an explanation. Most important, in
every instance make your comment be casual and strictly comment, not explanation nor a defense. And be mindful that
whether or not you are called upon to comment depends in
great measure on you and your own manner; thus, look on each
instance of it as a signal that you have let manner or other
changes creep into your abandonment of first names!

As your third move, cease identifying or referring to *yourself*
by your first name. If you call someone on the phone, don't say,
"This is George." Don't even say, "This is George Hayden."
Merely say, "This is Hayden." And do the same when you
answer the phone. Never say, "This is *Mister* Hayden," nor,
"This is *Doctor* Hayden," nor, "This is *Professor* Hayden," nor
even, "This is *Colonel* Hayden."

To carry it still farther, when you introduce yourself to
someone (or reply to their introduction), say, "I'm Hayden" or
"My name's Hayden." By doing these things in just this way, you
will, without any stuffed-shirtedness, cut off any first name
usage.

If you are female (in business or politics or a profession)
and seek to build yourself into a male-size self power, do
exactly the same. Every rule that applies to men applies also
to you when you seek to build yourself into such a power. Other
women before you have refused to acknowledge this and, as a
consequence, there has never been a self power giant among
them though the men have produced hundreds.

Commenting further, whether you are male or female, recognize this: People won't discontinue using your first name
instantly even though you discontinue using theirs! However,
depending on how naturally and matter-of-factly you make the
three moves, it will take only a few days to several weeks for
use of your first name to be automatically dropped by everyone.
And, if while making the three moves you make no slightest
other change in your relations with the people concerned, all
reaction against it will dissolve.

7. You have reached the fork in your road toward your aims

All three factors of the leveler technique are simple and easy, and they are essential to your building of self power, but as mentioned at the beginning of the previous section, you are probably reluctant to embark on them.

Once again it is pointed out to you,—self power is a much bigger and far different thing than the mere "getting along" with people. Its formulas and techniques are very different from those designed for winning friends, buttering customers, and the like, *and the two do not mix.*

Both are paths to popularity and toward accomplishing ends, but paths to different kinds of popularity and accomplishment. You are at a fork in the road and you must decide *now* whether the destination you desire can be reached by fellowship (courting people, flattering them, bending to them and establishing comradeship with them) or whether only self power can accomplish what you desire.

If the acceptance of you, and such favoring of you as that acceptance may bring, will make your life satisfying, then the easy way is to choose the path of fellowship and not try to build yourself into a self power. On the other hand, if your life can be made satisfying only by possession of the power to cause others to bend to you and perform for you, then you must abandon the fellowship path and build yourself into a self power. You cannot keep one foot in one path and one in the other for their directions are always opposite, never parallel.

Thus, if it is only through self power that life can be satisfying for you, you must now completely abandon every reluctance you may have toward the three moves of the leveler technique.

8. No matter what the success aim, self power is the greatest means

Every man who has ever built himself into a self power, and the greats who have chosen not to, will state that the decision that has just been forced on you is the most important one you will ever face because, when you make it, you will have determined upon a set course of life and a fixed relationship toward other beings.

A number of outstanding men were consulted regarding that decision and were asked how they thought you should be guided in the making of it. Most of the men were industrialists (because a greater number of people seek to achieve self power as such) but they also included an ex-President, a prominent clergyman-lecturer, a diplomat with thirty years in all parts of the globe, a scientist, a retired publisher, and a president of a retail chain. Despite their variety, they were in complete agreement as to what should guide your decision.

Each pointed out first that the overwhelming majority of men and women never face up to and make such a decision. The reason: Most people find life satisfying so long as they can attain something the same as or slightly better than the shelter, food, clothing and recreation that their original environment in life set as a standard for them, and this they can usually attain by merely "holding down" a job.

Next it was pointed out that, of the small percentage of persons who face up to and make the decision, most choose the fellowship path. The reason: Most people with ambition hunger first and foremost for recognition and acceptance, and consequently, consciously or unconsciously, look upon the prestige of recognition and acceptance as being more important to them than whatever other interests or beliefs or aims they may have; they measure their success more by the level at which they are recognized and accepted than by any other standard and, because of this, recognition and acceptance (not interests or beliefs or aims) are their driving force in whatever they do.

Third it was pointed out that the rare few of individuals who do make and abide by a decision to build themselves into a self power do so because they have a deep and compelling conviction that some interest or belief or aim of theirs surpasses all other considerations in importance.

As was further pointed out, the depth and strength and compulsion of that conviction is alone that which determines the strength and persistence of your drive toward self power and, unless you have such a conviction, you won't achieve self power and shouldn't strive for it. This does not mean you should forego it in entirety. It means that since you have no material aims you shouldn't strive toward an aimless wielding of it and should instead master its techniques and use them (not the fellowship path) to assure yourself a recognition and acceptance far superior to any the fellowship path can bring you. This because those techniques at the same time will cause you to feel and display a confidence and sincerity that are always at want in the fellowship path no matter how clever or successful you are with it.

As a conclusion, all expressed the opinion that if you are an individual who is capable of mastering and using the techniques of self power you should do so. The reason? It is simply this: Use of the techniques of self power will bring you a higher degree of self respect, and attendant respect from others, than is achievable by any other means.

9. Give the leveler technique extra time and heed

The leveler technique, because it is your power generating technique, must be in full operation before you attempt to go on to any others. All three factors of it are of equal importance, and unless you have all three in operation, it itself isn't in operation.

The worst mistake you could make at this point would be to jump ahead into the next steps of self power without taking time out to think the leveler technique through carefully. Begin with the five foundation stones that led you to it and firmly fix in your mind the separation that is essential to your getting along with people while putting the leveler technique into operation. Unless your training through life has been very different from that of most people, the effecting of the separation is going to be difficult for you, but you must take time to make it!

If you are going on to the other steps of self power, you must start your power generating before you do so. You must, in a definite and particular way, make people more aware of you and make yourself more aware of your individuality. Doing that will start your power generating and the leveler technique is your means of doing it. Give it all the time and attention it needs! (People who haven't, have sometimes made fools of themselves.) Make certain you understand why it is essential, and make very sure you know the why and how of all three of its factors.

10. Points worth special attention

1. Courtesy, respect, deference, politeness and manners are necessary in getting along with others.

2. Submissiveness must never be a characteristic of these relations with others.

3. Courtesy means but according graceful and tactful considerateness; being considerate of people willingly and kindly, not duteously or grumpily.

4. Respect means but acknowledging people and being cognizant of them and whatever individuality they possess.

5. Deference means but showing a regard for people's opinions, knowledge, authority, abilities, and the like; giving notice to these and making due and proper allowance for the other having them.

6. Politeness means but practicing a cultured regard for the status, actions, customs and beliefs of another consistent with the place and occasion; doing what good breeding calls for in the circumstance.

7. Manners mean but deporting yourself in a self-respectful way; deportment that is not offensive, rude or censurable; deportment governed by propriety and never guilty of lack of considerateness for others.

8. The purpose of the leveler technique is to raise your level, not reduce that of others.

9. Never use sir or its equivalents in addressing or answering others; use names or titles, in a brief sentence.

10. Abandon first name usage so as to prompt others to not address or refer to you by yours.

11. If life to be satisfying for you demands the power to cause others to bend to and perform for you, then self power is the only path to accomplishment.

12. A deep and compelling conviction that some interest or belief or aim of yours surpasses all other considerations in importance is the only force that can drive you to full fruition of self power.

13. Whether or not you go on to building yourself into a self power, use of the techniques of self power will bring you greater recognition, acceptance, respect, and self respect, than is achievable by any other means.

4

HOW TO MAKE ALL PEOPLE CONSCIOUS OF YOU

You must pull people's attention to make them consciously notice you.

Your initial pull force must be an instantly apparent distinctive individuality.

The only individuality that has the needed pull force is a self power attitude.

The see-and-be technique gives you your self power attitude.

Your self power attitude makes all people consciously notice you.

Shedding submissiveness and establishing a new relationship with people about you has made you a different person. It has given you a lift that has made you more of an individual. The people around you sense the change and it has given them a greater awareness of you. But that isn't enough. What you need now is to make them and *all* people very definitely and newly conscious of you.

1. You must use self power as your attention-getter

To make people conscious of you, you need to attract people's attention to you. That is a fact you can't escape. Whether you be a stranger in a crowd or be a day-to-day associate, people never fully consciously notice you unless you in some manner specially attract their attention to you.

Next, when you attract attention to yourself, people immediately see you in terms of their reaction to whatever you attract their attention with. If you attract their attention with actions, conduct, bearing, words or apparel that they view as undesirable (repulsive, ridiculous, ill-bred, etc.) they regard you yourself as being that very quality. Likewise, if you attract their attention with a commendable quality, they immediately see you as well-bred, gracious, intelligent, or whatever the quality is. Thus, *when people consciously notice you, they react, and what they see your attention-getter as being is what they see you as.*

And you can't escape a further fact either: How consciously people notice you (and notice you as) depends on how strongly and singularly your attention-getter attracts their attention to you.

With this in view, it now is time for you to turn your mind and thinking directly toward the first secret of self power. Remember, the first secret of self power (real personal power) is: *It strikes instantly!*

With that as your fourth fact (and no one can dispute that it is a fact), your next one is obvious to you. To make all people conscious of you, and make them see you as a self power quality, you must strongly and singularly use self power to attract people's attention to you!

But that brings you face to face with a difficulty: You haven't yet achieved self power.

2. You must build a technique that will show you as a power before you are one

You want to be a self power; you haven't yet built yourself into being one; but, in order to build yourself into being one, you have to start using self power *now*. In other words, here

and now, you have to start using something you don't have.
It can be done (just as you now use money you don't yet have),
and to achieve self power *you must do it.*

To do it, you're going to take the first secret of self power,
tear it apart, and then put it together piece by piece so that you
end up with a technique that will put that self power to use
for you as your attention-getter even though you don't yet
have it.

3. An instantly apparent distinctive individuality is the first pull

You know the first secret of self power and how it works and
what it means. You know that, whether people know you or
have never seen you before, it strikes them the instant they see
you. In other words, it does not depend on their knowing anything about you,—your name or title or affluence, or whether
you have any,—it projects self alone, but a special kind of self.

To strike favorably and instantly, and strike *all people,* as an
attention-getter it must have some quality that will make all
people instantly favorably conscious of you. Tear it apart.
When such power has smitten you,—when sight of some stranger
has forced you to notice him and prolong your notice and then
say, "That man *has* something!"—what first pulled you? One
thing: *An instantly apparent distinctive individuality.*

4. Building initial individuality is the most difficult task in building self power

Actually, three things happened before you felt compelled
to acknowledge "that man *has* something," but for now though,
you are concerned with only the first of these,—that instantly
apparent distinctive individuality. That is the particular thing
you want and must have, and your job now is to focus on it and
develop it.

Again, let's not be kidding you or anyone. The job of developing an instantly apparent distinctive individuality is the most difficult task you are going to face in your building of self power. It depends on your leveler technique being in full operation and then builds an added technique right within you. Because of these things, it requires that you prove to yourself that only one factor of your person can provide that so essential instantly apparent distinctive individuality.

5. The ingredients show what your something must be

As you look at the first secret of personal power, individuality is the main ingredient of it. Thus, first of all, there must be something about you that sets you apart from people in general. In other words, that something must cause you to be regarded particularly singly, not as one of any group, class or crowd.

Apparency is the next ingredient of it. Thus, whatever that something is that sets you apart from people, it must be clearly visible. It cannot be your voice, nor what you say, nor who you are, nor any other such,—it must be seeable and *clearly* seeable.

Distinctiveness is another ingredient of it. Thus, whatever that clearly visible something is that sets you apart from people, it must be markedly distinguishing. Said differently, the visible individuality must be of unusually singular character.

Instantness is the final ingredient. Thus, whatever that clearly visible markedly distinguishing something is that sets you apart from people, it must show itself instantly. Which means, it must always be in existence so that at every instant (not just at intervals) it is seeable. You can't "turn it on" when people see you,— you must have it *before* they see you.

You've put together the whole of what it must be,—a clearly visible markedly distinguishing something that shows itself always and instantly sets you apart from people. That's what it must be. Your job now is to find it and develop it.

6. Props can't be your "something"

Since the "something" must be always visible, it must of necessity exist in your above-the-shoulders area. If it failed to exist in that area it wouldn't be visible when you are standing in or moving along through a group or crowd. Neither would it be visible while you are seated in a theatre, at a desk, in a taxi, or many other places.

Before your mind dives into a whirlpool of beards, mustaches, eyeglasses, monocles, and all sorts of other things you might don as the "something above the shoulders," remind yourself that people have already tried all manner of such things and they never are the "something" you need to develop. In fact, when those or any other prop is an attention getter, *it, not you* is what people are conscious of.

7. If you use a prop, display it defyingly

Even while saying that, it must be acknowledged that many persons who have built themselves into giants of self power have included props (a distinctive form of beard or mustache or eyeglasses or monocle or hairstyle or cigarette holder or collar or something else) in their individuality, and that many of them, particularly political leaders, have included combinations of such items (as did Franklin D. Roosevelt, Winston Churchill, Adolf Hitler, and others). For some, unusual features nature bestowed on them became such props (as did those of John L. Lewis, Benito Mussolini, and others). But none of those persons used the props as their "something,"—all of them used the props only as a "trademark."

If you feel you need a prop to lean on in developing and putting forth the "something," go ahead and use one. But if you do, make sure it will be you, never a copy of someone else. And make sure you only use it to bolster your courage, not to get attention. A word of caution: If you do use a prop to bolster your courage, it must be sufficiently unusual to cause you to display it defyingly!

8. Only attitude can provide your "something"

In the words "display it defyingly" you have a further key to your "something". Let's take a closer look at it and pin it down.

Any physical features that are attention getters are but props, so your physical features (no matter how good or bad they are), can't be your something. With props and physical features thus ruled out, only two things are left to you as possibilities,— expression and attitude. The first of these is ruled out because, if it were ever to be constant, it would show you as lifeless. As a consequence, only one thing, attitude, can provide the "something" you must have. Now, focusing on attitude, let's set about the developing of your "something" attitude. And remember, *your attitude must be clearly visible, markedly distinguishing, and show itself always so as to instantly set you apart from people.*

9. Your self power attitude must be lived

All sorts of methods have been experimented with and tried in the teaching of the self power attitude. So far however, no method, other than that used in the past few pages, has ever been successful. And even it is not successful unless, by now, it has made you understand exactly what your "something" must be and why only attitude can provide it.

At this point you need to give recognition to another feature of self power. It is a *living* force and your personal power attitude must be a living thing, it can't be portrayed or acted. (The most conclusive proof of this is supplied by the fact that the best acting talent of the theatre and motion pictures has never been able to accurately portray it.)

To develop your personal power attitude you must beforehand have a feel for personal power and a feel of it generating. These you have from your leveler technique (if you have it in full operation). Next it requires that you feel yourself (a) immune to disparagement, (b) unfearful of challenge, and (c) beneath nothing and no one.

10. The see-and-be technique

Since the leveler technique has already given you the first of what you require, you can put your full attention now on the second requirement of your personal power attitude.

Dozens of methods have been invented and expounded for the achieving of this second requirement and you probably have even tried some of them. In the main, all of them follow one pattern: They tell you to sell yourself on being immune to disparagement (on a "sticks and stones, etc." basis); to sell yourself on being unfearful of challenge (on a "because defeat, not challenge, is the thing to fear," etc., basis); and to "sell yourself" on other things. If you have tried such methods, you know they don't work. In theory they're fine, but what you need is a simpler and surer method,—one that *does* work.

The only simple and sure technique so far found that truly brings forth your self power attitude is the see-and-be technique. So far as is known, everyone who ever built himself into being a self power succeeded only after using it!

The see-and-be technique has no fancy theory, no sell yourself, and no hocus-pocus. It simply says this to you: You're going to build yourself into a self power, a very special kind of power. You know this, you've set your mind on it, and you, in your mind, already visualize that particular self power.

You visualize the self power, you visualize what you will be when you have it, you visualize yourself as fitted to self power, you visualize yourself as someone all people will notice, an individual whom people will regard favorably and admiringly, whom they will want to know, want to please, and want to enjoy a bond with. Your mind's eyes are on that vision. They see the individual in that vision as one who is immune to the tongues and opinions of the world, as one unfearful of any challenge, and as one who is beneath nothing and no one.

Your mind's eyes see that vision as the individual you will someday be. In other words, *they see the attributes and qualities* and they superimpose you on them. What you must now do is make your mind's eyes reverse that, see you and superimpose the attributes and qualities on you!

That means simply this, your mind must assign those attributes and qualities to you beforehand, make you live them, for unless you do so (live them first) you never can acquire them in fact. Therefor, instead of looking at the qualities and attributes, *look at yourself*, and see yourself (not a vision of you) as having those attributes and qualities. I know you don't have them yet, you know you don't have them, but no one else does. So, live them as if you did have them! It's the same as if you aspired to a newer and finer home, and I told you to put a down payment on it and have it,—I know you don't own it yet, you know it, but the world at large that sees you in it doesn't know it, and so you "live" your home as if you already *do* own it, and in the meantime you little by little pay for it and finally do own it.

You are going to own self power. You've made your down payment, so live it now! Quit being whatever you are, quit seeing what you are,—see and be *only what you are going to be.*

11. All people are conscious of your self power attitude

The whole secret and trick of the success of the technique lies in the fact that, when you see yourself as you are going to be, you *are* immune to disparagement, you *are* unfearful of challenge, and you immediately are beneath nothing and no one. The result is, you instantly look out at the world differently, see people differently, bear yourself differently, and resultantly are seen differently by everyone.

Without effort or conscious attention to it on your part,

your head carries itself so as always to be looking at the horizon. You don't make it do it,—it does it automatically.

Similarly, without effort or conscious attention on your part, your eyes are clearer and more seeing. And your mind is more awake! Your periods of daydreaming come almost to an end and mental preoccupation, when you have any, no longer clouds your eyes or face.

These are the things that are a self power attitude. These are the things other people do not have. Consequently, as they develop in you they give you *your* self power attitude. And as you get it, all people are conscious of it. It strikes them instantly,—for it is a clearly visible markedly distinguishing attitude that instantly sets you apart from people!

12. You've begun the pulling of others toward you

Your self power attitude pulls attention. Strangers notice you, and notice you favorably. People who herebefore saw you without noticing you suddenly are approvingly conscious of you each time they see you. And your fellow workers and associates suddenly, and somewhat wonderingly, see you with different eyes and are newly conscious of you. You feel all these things, but the most important thing is that *people are feeling you.*

You've come a long way, and in a remarkably short time. You already have completed the biggest and most difficult step in the building of yourself into a self power. All who have self power will confirm that you never achieve self power unless you complete that step but, when you do complete it, self power is already only inches from your grasp!

The magnitude of that step sometimes hides its purpose. Remind yourself of what that purpose is: *To strike instantly, and strike all people, so as to make all people conscious there is self power within you.* It is the step that begins the pulling of people toward you.

13. Points worth special attention

1. People never fully consciously notice you unless you specially attract their attention.

2. People see you as whatever they see that attracts their attention to you.

3. How consciously people notice you depends on how strongly and singularly you attract their attention.

4. To strike people's consciousness instantly and with force you must have an instantly apparent distinctive individuality.

5. It must set you apart from people, be clearly visible, be markedly distinguishing, and always be in existence.

6. Props can't provide it; props attract attention to themselves, not to you, unless your individuality is more striking than they are.

7. A self power attitude is the only thing that can provide you with the essential individuality.

8. Your self power attitude must be alive; it can't be acted or faked.

9. Your self power attitude requires that you have a feel for self power, that you feel it generating, that you feel immune to disparagement, that you feel unfearful of challenge, and that you feel beneath nothing and no one.

10. The see-and-be technique is the simple and sure means to a self power attitude.

11. As your self power attitude develops you feel it, and all people are conscious of it.

5

HOW TO MAKE PEOPLE WANT TO KNOW YOU

Holding people's attention requires much beyond the get-ting of it.

People never give you their interest; you must pull it.

You want to pull all people, not merely some class or group.

The "tune 'em in" technique pulls all people's interest.

Causing people to tune-in to you pulls them all toward wanting to know you and get along with you.

People's consciousness of you must lead to their wanting to know you. Only in that way can you step closer and closer to self power. You must make strangers want to know you, and at the same time you must make acquaintances want to know you better.

1. You must keep people's shells open

Arresting the attention of people, pulling their consciousness to you in their first glimpse of you, is exceedingly important, but self power demands a lot more than that you merely make people conscious of you.

First of all, except for people who live in isolated places,

42

all people wear a shell that guards them against being conscious of every individual they see or encounter. (If they didn't, they could never venture out of their homes into the masses of humanity that are everywhere! Their all-noticing would make them forever as hopelessly and frighteningly bewildered as the "boy from nowhere" dropped suddenly in the heart of a metropolis, and would drive them toward insanity.) As a consequence, that shell keeps them from being more than but superficially conscious of even their associates and daily contacts. Only when there is something strikingly unusual about someone do their shells open.

Any strikingly unusual thing can open the shells, but in your case, you are using your self power attitude to open them. What you must do now is provide something that will keep them open. Unless you do, the shells snap shut with as much suddenness as you opened them. But with the right trick or technique, you can stop that from happening.

2. Only interest will keep people's shells open

Even though you are already over the rough spots, throughout these twenty steps you are going to have to face a lot of cold, hard facts and right here is where you need to face another of them: Merely getting people's attention doesn't make them interested enough to *give* it to you; when you yank their attention to yourself you have to immediately pull their interest— or *wham!*—their attention is lost.

If people's shells made noises as they open and snap shut you'd be hearing clack-clacks all day, for all sorts of things get attention momentarily. Your self power attitude is just one of the many things. An unusual female, an unusually stout person, an unusually crazy hat, all catch attention,—but then, clack-clack, they lose it *unless they also pull interest.*

The female who catches attention has various means for pulling various kinds of interest, and you do too. Some of her means are designed to pull an interest that will make certain

categories of people want to know her. You, however, don't
want to pull interest from just certain categories,—you need
to have *all* people to want to know you. Her purposes aim at
groups, but your purpose is self power, and self power isn't fully
effective unless *all* people recognize it.

3. The "tune 'em in" technique

To make all people want to know you, you must pull the
interest of all people. And to pull the interest of all people,
once you have their attention on you, you must immediately
dangle something before them that will readily appeal to every
man, woman and child. Only one thing will do that,—*a definite evidencing to the world of yourself as "tuned-in" to
it.*

You must show the world you have an alive awareness of it.
You must make your face, your countenance, show people
that your mind and ears and eyes are actively conscious of the
world as a whole and of people in particular.

What that means is, don't be dead-pan. Don't let your face
show you as occupied with only your thoughts. When you are
among people, on the street, in an office, in an elevator, in a
restaurant, anywhere at all, make yourself give attention to the
fact that people *are* there and that things are going on, being
done, or happening. Don't just be subconsciously aware, be
alively aware. Make your eyes take in people and things, make
your ears hear people and things, and your face will show that
you *are* seeing and hearing all that is about you. One sentence
can sum it all: *Never allow yourself the luxury or refuge of
preoccupation when you are among people!*

Automatically, when you blank out preoccupation you acquire and have *and show* an alive awareness of all that is about
you. The world sees you as an individual whose mind and
ears and eyes are conscious of it,—as an individual who is
tuned in.

Quite definitely, when people see you as tuned-in to the
world, you spark people to a curious interest in you. And, when

they see you as not just tuned-in to the world but as tuned-in to people too, their interest expands and makes them want to kindredly tune-in to you.

What does it take? Most of all it takes wakefulness; looking awake and being awake, never preoccupied. Next it takes little things; a seeing smile in your eyes, or doing your seeing, not with coldness, but with a smile or warmth or interest in your eyes,—and giving notice to the existence of people with a smile or a nod.

By being awake and looking awake, and wearing a seeing smile in your eyes, you distinguish yourself as far apart from the ordinary. And when you blend this into your self power attitude, people immediately see you as that special one in a million that everyone would like to be.

4. Build on your tune-in whenever you can

For people to see you as tuned-in to them doesn't require that you be tuned-in to each of them individually. Just seeing you as tuned-in to people as a whole makes all people feel you are in some manner tuned-in to them individually or readily would be. However, if they ever see your tune-in give notice to individuals, they are pulled even stronger toward tuning in to you.

For example: If, without need of words, your eyes show you as giving kindly notice to individuals that people as a whole take for granted or disregard (porters, bellhops, ticket-takers, ushers, typists, clerks, cleaning people, etc.), all people immediately feel inside themselves that your notice extends to everyone, including them.

To build your tune-in to a maximum, let your eyes, without need of words, show you as openly giving favorable regard to things that identify with individuals. For instance, when people see your eyes (as you hurry, stroll, stand or sit) regarding an individual's child, work, possession or something else approvingly, they (even though maybe envious) are pulled more strongly toward you.

As a final step toward building your tune-in to a maximum, let your eyes show that you *hear* people, particularly when they address you. And then, when people put forth their ideas, theories, problems and opinions to you, whether you approve of them or not, and even if you don't comment, let your eyes be showing that you at least are hearing them.

5. Every technique has a success secret or trick

Every self power technique, like the techniques of punting a football, rowing a boat, or doing anything else, has some trick that its success depends on. Focus your attention on the trick in any technique and the remaining factors of the technique (once known) will usually take care of themselves.

In the "tune 'em in" technique, the whole trick lies in your being wakefully enough aware of the world and people for your wakeful awareness to immediately show. It can't wait for you to voice it, or to convince people of it otherwise. They must *see it,* immediately your self power attitude has drawn their attention to you.

Don't practice it in front of a mirror,—and don't try to fake it by darting your eyes around or using any other form of exaggerated alertness. Simply be wakefully seeing at all times. If you are, your eyes and mind and ears will be tuned-in to the world and people, and people will see it. Then, automatically, their seeing it will "tune 'em in" to you.

Take a good look at every self power you ever see. He *never* allows himself the luxury or refuge of preoccupation when he is among people because he already knows what you too must learn and constantly heed: The "tune 'em in" technique is the strongest "people puller" in every self power's bag of tricks!

6. Self power depends on people always seeing you as being whatever you are, never as seeming it

As a final word on success of the "tune 'em in" technique,— if it and your self power attitude are genuine, there won't be any problem of unwanted emotions showing themselves and neither will there be any temptation for you to be improperly demonstrative or to pretend feelings you don't have.

Be mindful of this: You are building yourself into a self power. For you to be one, people from the very first must see you as genuine in whatever you are, good or bad. *People must always see you as being, never as seeming.*

Your own experiences will prevent you from disputing the fact that people are always wary of anyone they see as seeming, even when he seems a saint,—and yet people are always fascinated by the one they see as being, even when their mind's eye sees him with horns and a trident.

7. People tune-in to you because they want to know you and get along with you

Getting along with people is always important, as pointed out at the very beginning, but, as was also pointed out, one of your objectives of self power is to draw people to you in a manner that will cause *them* to want to get along with *you*. The "tune 'em in" technique is your first big step in that direction.

Just as the see-and-be technique has made your associates and acquaintances newly conscious of you, so has the "tune 'em in" technique made them newly interested in you. As a result of their new interest, you find them regarding you differently, approaching you differently, and even speaking to you differently. Already they are extending you new and little courtesies.

As you observe and feel these things, don't make the fatal error of reacting to them as you would have yesterday. Don't be flattered by them,—and don't feel that they call for reciprocity! Those people are, unconsciously maybe, beginning to court you the same as you only a yesterday or two ago were courting other people.

Tomorrow, as a self power, you will be courted in some manner by all people. React to those who begin the courting today as you know you must react when you are courted tomorrow. Be receptive, even appreciative, but neither flattered

nor given to condescension. Accept their courting as a trib-
ute.

8. Points worth special attention

1. As you make people conscious of you, you must pull their interest
toward you immediately.

2. Pulling of their interest can't be left to chance; you must have a
positive tool for pulling it.

3. The tool must pull all people, not just certain types or groups of
people.

4. The "tune 'em in" technique is the only tool that pulls all people
everywhere.

5. Your being tuned-in to the world and people will "tune 'em in" to
you.

6. In any technique, focus your attention on the trick of it and its other
factors will usually take care of themselves.

7. The whole trick of the "tune 'em in" technique lies in your being
wakefully enough aware so that your tune-in immediately shows to all
people.

8. Your tune-in must be genuine and truly wakefully seeing at all
times.

9. To assure success with it, never allow yourself the luxury or refuge
of preoccupation when you are among people.

10. The "tune 'em in" technique is the strongest "people puller" in
your bag of tricks.

11. Be what you show yourself as, don't seem to be it.

12. React to people today as you will need to tomorrow, not as you
would have yesterday.

6

HOW TO PRIME AND WARM UP PEOPLE

To hold people's interest you must warm them to responsiveness.

You must warm all people, not merely a goodly percentage.

The beam-it-back technique is the only sure means of
warming all people.

The beam-it-back technique makes people responsive to
the self power with which you caught their attention.

With your self power attitude you have caught people's
attention. All people, as they catch sight of you, consciously
notice you instantly. And, as they notice you, you are immediately capturing their interest. You are keeping their shells
open. Now, while you have their shells open, you need to draw
them more, dangling a little extra something that will warm
them to you and make them come out of their shells expectantly
and relyingly.

1. Standard tricks for warming people can't serve your purpose

Once you have people's attention and interest there are all
sorts of ways to warm them. Salesmen, pitch-men, entertainers

49

and speakers have their own bags of tricks for doing it. Politicians, lawyers and chairmen have still other bags of tricks. And girls have their tricks for it and boys have theirs. Even gossipers have their bags of tricks for warming people. And you, no matter who or what you have been, have used tricks for doing it too.

In every instance those tricks follow one set pattern. While the attention and interest are fresh and alive, actions or manner or words quickly imply that something is promised (a bargain, a handout, a disclosure, or anything else that the interested might "go for").

Those tricks work. You've used them and you know they work,—but you also know they work only on a goodly percentage of people, not on all people. Therefor, no matter how good those tricks are, and no matter how clever you have been at using them, none of them can serve your present purpose. As a fast maturing self power you need to warm *all* people, not just a goodly percentage of them.

Even as it is pointed out that those tricks can't serve your present purposes it must be acknowledged that many self powers have made use of them. However, you are reminded that, though they used them, they did not use them in the process of becoming self powers. They used them after they became self powers and used them mainly because their old inferiority fears and lack of confidence overtook them. As a consequence, once they started using them their power lost its strength as a self power and became entirely dependent on promising and promising, to more and more people.

2. Use a technique other people can't use

Since you need to warm all people, not just a goodly percentage, you need a technique that will do it without implying any promise. In addition, you need to make certain that you abandon your old tricks completely and never let even a small bit of them mix in with your self power. If they do mix in, they'll dilute your self power and your self element in it will give way more and more toward a promise element and lead to futile dependence on promise power.

There are two means by which you can warm people without implying or making promises, but one of these is useless to you. The means that is useless to you is one that in the main calls for you to show yourself as overly attentive to people (exaggeratedly courteous, polite, gracious, etc.). Since such would return you to traits of liegemanship and the courting of people, and would thus nullify the whole of your advance toward self power, you don't dare use it or anything bearing any similarity to it.

Because of all these things, there is only one means left that you can use to prime and warm people to you. However, your one means is a simple and sure one, and it works on all people. In addition, it has another big, big factor that enormously increases its value to you,—*other people can't use it!*

The means you are going to use to prime and warm people is the beam-it-back technique. It will work for you, and on all people, but it won't work for anyone who doesn't have the self power attitude and the world and people tune-in.

3. The beam-it-back technique

When you catch people's attention and capture their interest, people look at you deliberately. They don't give you a passing or casual look,—they put their eyes directly on you and give you a *deliberate* look.

When other people are given a deliberate look either of several things happens. They self-centeredly fail even to notice it; they notice it but purposely ignore it; they try to ignore it and can't and become overly self-conscious; they brazen it by staring back; they are bothered by it and show resentment of it; or, they are flattered by it and openly invite more of it (as does a girl who, flattered by interest in her legs, exposes more of them).

In your case, you are wakeful and tuned in and so you are *not* unaware of the deliberate looks that are turned on you. You need those deliberate looks and you need to be aware of them, so don't resent them or be bothered by them and *don't ignore them.* Accept them, but don't be flattered by them. And above all, *don't stare back at the people who give them to you.* Instead, heed their deliberate looks by deliberately and fleetingly beaming a recognizing twinkle (*not* a grin or smile) at them.

You know that your self power attitude and your tune-in are catching attention and pulling interest. You therefor know that all people are looking at you deliberately. Because of this, *you do not wait* to feel or see such a look,—you assume every face in your range of vision is giving you one and *you fleetingly beam a deliberately recognizing twinkle at every face your eyes encounter.*

4. The recognizing twinkle is the trick

Your past experiences have led you to believe that it is difficult to warm people and that only the most expert promising and clever attentiveness can better a two-out-of-twenty batting average. And that's true, where those techniques are the ones that are used. However, when you use the beam-it-back technique, people warm easily and quickly and, without any need of expertness or cleverness, you bat a thousand every time.

Your success trick is a simple one. All it requires is that you fleetingly but deliberately look at everyone as if you recognize him or her! And that you put in your look of recognition that same twinkle you always have had on seeing and recognizing someone you regard pleasantly.

5. Your recognizing twinkle makes people responsive

In deliberately beaming a recognizing twinkle at people, you aren't pretending to know them,—you are accepting and giving recognition to their interest. And that is what they themselves see it as. Thus, and because they see it as that, they see you as approachable and receptive,—a person without fences,—a distinctively unaloof and not distant individual. More than that, they see you as responsive.

Those qualities are exceedingly rare. To convince yourself of this, and of why the beam-it-back technique works so magically, search through all the crowds of persons you see each day and try to find one who has those qualities.

Those qualities increase and enhance the distinctiveness that has caught the notice and interest of people. They show you as an individual who has dropped his bars and opened himself to people. And because people see you as such, they drop their bars in that segment of their fence that opens toward you. In short, *they become responsive to that self power of yours that caught their attention.*

6. Recognize everyone your eyes ever touch

Any technique, to be a good one, must infallibly accomplish its purpose and be simple enough to be readily usable by everyone for whom it is intended. Every technique in these pages meets those standards. When any, like the beam-it-back technique, is exceedingly simple, don't regard its lack of intricacy as a lack of value.

The beam-it-back technique, like all the others, is essential to your building of self power. It has already been well emphasized that the "tune 'em in" technique is your strongest "people puller." It needs equal emphasis that the beam-it-back technique is, not your strongest, but your only usable trick for warming people to responsiveness. Never be lax in mindfulness that once you have people's interest you must warm them to you,—cause them to be responsive to the self power that caught their notice. And impress indelibly on your mind that *the beam-it-back technique is your only means for accomplishing this.*

Use it! Make your recognizing twinkle recognize! And make it recognize everyone your eyes ever touch.

7. Points worth special attention

1. You must warm people to you to pull them out of their shells.

2. Dangling the right "extra something" brings them from their shells expectantly and relyingly.

3. Using standard warming tricks (promissive tricks) would defeat your purpose.

4. The beam-it-back technique infallibly warms all people and makes them responsive.

5. Beaming recognition is the trick.

6. Beam your recognizing twinkle at everyone your eyes touch.

7. Your recognizing twinkle shows you distinctively unaloof and implies you are responsive.

8. Showing your bars as down makes people drop theirs.

9. Through the beam-it-back technique you capture the essential initial responsiveness to your self power.

10. Make your recognizing twinkle recognize and use it constantly; it's the only "people warmer" that is usable with self power.

7

HOW TO PULL FORTH FRIENDLINESS

You must pull friendliness, not wait for it.

Put your aim and effort on the first inch of friendliness.

The "first inch" technique makes your first sound pull friendliness.

The "talk up front" technique keeps friendliness coming
your way.

Talking naturally and adequately but sparingly makes
friendliness come easier.

Leaving talkativeness to others puts extra insurance on
friendliness.

In quick succession you have snared attention, pulled interest
and drawn approval. Figuratively, you've made people leave
the gate open to you. And you've done it all without uttering
a word! You're a man of whom the world is already saying,
on sight alone, "That man *has* something!" Now you need to
take the next step and pull forth friendliness so you can start
pocketing the world.

1. In seconds, and without a word,
you open people

Glance back a moment at the steps you've just completed,
specifically the last three.

Your self power attitude smacks people the instant they see you and in that same instant compels them to consciously notice you. Immediately they notice you, *in that first second or two of their sight of you,* your tune-in strikes and in those same seconds forces them to become interested in you. Then, *in those seconds when their interest is at peak and curious,* your recognizing twinkle dissolves all their speculativeness and makes them leave themselves open to you.

It has taken three chapters to give you the techniques and tricks for doing all that but it only takes you fifteen to sixty seconds to accomplish it. Being a self power you amazingly accomplish all of it in the first seconds of anyone's sight of you and before you utter a word!

2. To pull people, you need something to pull on

Now that you have people open to you, you need to draw them a little more toward you. Quite truly, their gates are open and you could go toward them,—but that is wrong for two reasons.

If you, figuratively speaking, go toward people (that is, make the first advance), no matter how wide they've left the gates open, they instinctively switch to en garde. The fact that *you* made the advance creates an expectancy that it has a purpose that may be more favorable to you than to them.

The other reason why it would be wrong for you to go toward people is that to do so would be to disregard your objective. Your objective is to *make people move toward you.*

Thus, if you are going to now draw people a little more toward you, you must do it by pulling them. And if you are going to pull them, you must awaken something in them that you can pull on.

3. Awaken and pull on people's friendliness

Sympathy, pity, charitableness, generosity and all manner of other feelings are things you could pull on but nothing of that kind could be used to pull people to where you need them. Those feelings reach down. They always are extended to persons seen as needy (even if needy only of such feelings). You want to awaken and pull on something that will reach out or up to you, not down to you.

Normally, the hardest thing to awaken and pull on is friendliness, but friendliness is the *only* thing you can pull on to get people to where you can pocket them. People rarely leave friendliness out where you can grab it. What you need now therefor is a technique for awakening friendliness and for seizing and pulling on it to pull people toward you.

4. Your technique must aim at the first inch of friendliness

One of the oriental philosophers has been translated as saying, "The first inch of anything is the most essential one but it is the most ignored because it is the hardest to pull forth." Someone else translated that as, "Spend every needed effort on pulling forth the first inch for, once it is within your grasp, the rest pulls forth easily."

You can ignore those as philosophy if you want to, but don't ignore them as sound advice on the pulling forth of friendliness. Nothing could be truer than that once you put forth the proper effort and get that first inch of friendliness in your grasp, the rest of it is pulled forth easily!

Because this is so true, any technique you use must concentrate on getting the first inch and on getting it with the first sound you utter.

5. The "first inch" technique

When you have people's attention and interest, and have them open to you, the manner of your putting forth of your first sound has an instantaneous and magical effect on others.

Though you (and people themselves) may not be aware of it, people subconsciously anticipate what your first sound will be.

As a consequence, you (as an individual) are greatly measured by how your first sound measures up to the anticipation of it.

If your first sound falls short of being the kind of sound people anticipate "will come from you," you lose them instantly. If it doesn't fall short but is only "as anticipated," people see you too as only "what they expected" and, though they may remain open to you, they are indifferently open to you,—you aren't anything "too special."

On the other hand, if your first sound is beyond their anticipation, and particularly when it is high beyond their anticipation, definitely and surprisingly pleasing to them, they instantly take the wraps off their friendliness and push their friendliness toward you. They give you an "inch" that is ten yards long!

For your first sound to get that first inch, the sound must be right. Whether you sing, speak or whistle it, *it must please.* To emphasize this, fix in your mind that there are thousands of things it can't be (raucous, harsh, boisterous, jovial, throaty, grumpy, squeaky, etc.) and only one thing it *can* be,—clearly and livingly pleasant.

Whether you are saying hello, good evening, thank you, ladies and gentlemen, fellow stockholders, Mr. Customer, or what you're saying, the sound must issue from a proper background and have a distinct quality. Thus you must equally and simultaneously give attention to two things, the sound and the background from which it issues.

Like the sound, there are many things the background can't be and only one thing it can be if it is to accomplish its purpose. It must be an awake face that looks like it readily could smile. It should therefor be the face of your recognizing twinkle.

The sound itself must have a quality that is a blend of a clear and living and pleasant speaking manner so that it will issue forth as the clearly and livingly pleasant sound that is "the only thing" it *can* be.

This isn't quite so difficult as it at first might seem. Several tips can help you. First, don't let your initial word be one that begins with an "o" sound. That is, avoid uttering oak, ode, odious, ocean, ochre, old, omen, over, etc., as your first sound. To understand why, look in a mirror, put a smile on your face, and then try to not disturb the smile while you say oak or any other word that begins with an "o" sound. Such words erase every trace of a smile from your face.

As a second tip, words that begin with the letter "b" should be avoided as your initial word. Words like boy, borrow, bundle, burn, etc., erase all traces of a smile except when you consciously make a deliberate effort to hold your smile. This too your mirror can prove to you.

As a third tip, be watchful for and avoid (as initial word) any of the few dozen other words that are difficult or impossible to say through a smile (wrong, wrought, gargle, grease, etc.) because these, like the "o" sound and letter "b" words, distort your all-important background and thus lessen the effect of your initial utterance no matter how perfect it might be otherwise.

As a fourth tip, watch your hearers' eyes as you utter your first sounds. This you should be doing anyway, but as you do it notice whether their eyes liven with interest. If they don't, if they remain unchanged or cloud, you aren't scoring. On the other hand, if they do liven with interest you are scoring, and that first inch is there for you. Grasp it!

6. The trick lies in not letting your first sound change you

Never make the mistake of regarding the uttering of your first sound as being too small a detail to be worthy of so much special attention. Actually, it is so important a one that many wielders of personal power pay more attention to it than to any other. (Franklin D. Roosevelt paid such obvious attention to it that he for a time made the detail and the technique famous.

To refresh your mind on this, and especially on his "My friends" opening, listen to a recording of any of his "fireside chats," particularly those of the middle thirties.)

The trick that makes the technique work may give you some difficulty, mainly because it calls on you to break an old habit. It is simply this: As you utter that first sound, don't let your manner or expression change. (Commonly your manner and expression change the instant you start to speak,—or sing or whistle.)

As has already been emphasized, your recognizing twinkle must continue and be a background for your first sound, but if you are to achieve maximum effectiveness as you pull that all important first inch of friendliness, your self power attitude and your tune-in also must continue and not be disturbed nor distorted.

Put your time and effort on getting that first sound out without letting it change you. Lick that and you've got the first inch.

7. The "talk up front" technique

With the first inch of friendliness in your grasp you shouldn't have any trouble with holding it and pulling the rest. And that's what you must do for you must keep friendliness coming your way.

Here again, the technique is simple but it calls for changing an old habit.

The "talk up front" technique requires that you continue to talk through your recognizing twinkle while using the front of your mouth exclusively. *It can be done.* However, if you, like most people, are in the habit of talking from your throat or molars, you will probably need to go off alone somewhere to practice and master it.

It should be pointed out that "talking up front" means "forming the words" up front, nothing more. If you have culti-vated good speaking and singing "air volume" habits, such as "breathing from the diaphragm" and storing air there and issuing it from there, continue them. They'll help you do a better job with the "talk up front" technique. Similarly, if you have had speech or voice training, such training has emphasized that clear pronunciation, pronouncing with distinctness of articulation, is best achieved by making full use of the lips, teeth and tongue tip as you enunciate, and this habit should be cultivated; the "talk up front" technique is nothing more than an overemphasis of and overattentiveness to this detail in your speaking.

If it were habit for people to properly enunciate in all their speaking there would be no need to put forth the "talk up front" technique, but such isn't the case. People as a whole (even those who are attentive to their articulation in delivering speeches) commonly pay little heed to where and how they form their words in business, social, casual or everyday conversation. Because of this, they lapse into habits that make little use of their lips, teeth and tongue tip and form their words mostly in the back of their mouth ("off their molars") or in their throats. Some even use the nasal passages. If you are a ventriloquist, such habits are necessary, but if you are to be a self power they must be avoided. Because they do not form your words "where they can be seen" they prevent your words from being fully accepted as frankly and openly spoken. And your words must be so accepted if you are to pull forth the added friendliness that is your purpose.

As all of the foregoing makes clear, the trick of the "talk up front" technique lies in making yourself talk as fully as possible with your lips, teeth and tongue tip. There is nothing difficult in it, it calls only for attentiveness to doing so. However, if even that sounds like work, remind yourself of this: It is far easier and simpler to master the trick of talking in the front of your mouth than it is to ever pull friendliness without it.

Make "talking up front" a new and constant habit. If you do

that, and don't relinquish your self power traits while doing it, you'll keep on pulling the friendliness!

8. Talk when you need but don't be talkative

From here on, your manner and voice and words are going to be noticed more as being whatever they are. If you don't stiffen (and many people *do* stiffen at this point) it will be an easy matter for you to continue putting yourself forth pleasingly. If you do stiffen, find amusement in the fact that you have,—and simply smile and start over again.

Whenever you speak or converse, or people speak to you, look at them as if they mattered. Never look through them or look at them blankly. And direct your voice to them as if it is meant for them.

Contrary to popular excuses people make about voices, no matter what kind of voice you have, you can make it a pleasing one and use it in a pleasing manner. Your vocal cords govern what kind of voice you have and, no matter how high or low your voice is, it is only harsh, gruff, strident, squeaky, or anything else irritating, when you tense the muscles it uses and cause it to be such. Keep its muscles relaxed. Nervousness, fright, excitement and many other emotions can cause almost anyone to tense the muscles, and tenseness thus caused is not easily avoided. On the other hand, tensing the muscles when speaking is nothing more than habit for many people, and habit tenseness can be avoided. Avoid it, even seeking medical advice if necessary, and then don't let your voice be louder than necessary, and always "talk up front."

Let your voice come out naturally (never force it out) and it will be even more pleasing. Here again your "air volume" habits, if you have any, can help you. And lastly, use your voice sparingly,—not talkatively. Leave the talkativeness to the other persons,—the more you do so the more of their friendliness will come your way.

9. Points worth special attention

1. Ignore the fact that you have people open to you and deal with them on a basis of your being open to them.

2. Your objective is to move people toward you, not to move toward them.

3. Awaken their friendliness for it is the best thing you can use to pull them toward you.

4. Concentrate all your efforts first on pulling forth the first inch of their friendliness.

5. By using the "first inch" technique, get their first inch of friendliness with the first sound you utter.

6. Make your first sound exceed, not just equal, their anticipation; make it clearly and livingly pleasant.

7. Don't let your first word be one that can't easily be said through a smile.

8. The trick of the "first inch" technique lies in not letting your first sound change you.

9. Use the "talk up front" technique to pull more and more friendliness and keep it coming your way.

10. Don't relinquish your self power traits while you speak or converse.

11. If you get off stride and stiffen, simply smile and start over again.

12. As you speak or people speak to you, look at them as if they mattered.

13. When you need to talk, talk naturally and adequately, but sparingly.

14. Always leave talkativeness to others.

8

HOW TO LISTEN AGGRESSIVELY

Listening can be wielded as a weapon against those who
use talking as a weapon.

How others talk to you can be controlled by your listening
manner and techniques.

The "lend" technique is your key weapon.

The "fact-finder" technique wards off those who seek to
nullify your status.

The "servilizor" technique pushes back those who would
put themselves above you.

The "warp" technique twists astray those who try to exercise power over you.

Others can be controlled through controlling their attitudes
and thinking with your manner and word skill.

By being able to pull forth an initial friendliness (instead of
having to rely on only that which ordinarily gravitates to you)
you are already controlling and pocketing people. Figuratively,
you now have the ball. Your next job is to tighten your grasp
on it, not drop it, and start going toward your goal with it.

1. Instead of "just listening," you must wield listening as a weapon

At the completion of your last previous step you were ad-
monished to leave talkativeness to others. That is a must if you

are to achieve a maximum of self power. However, in leaving talkativeness to others you must also make them *reach up* toward you. If you don't, you'll soon find that your letting them be talkative also lets them assume or pretend to a superiority.

Whether you have heretofore been aware of it or not, talking is a weapon, and people will seize the chance to wield it as such every time you allow them the opportunity. When people wield it as a weapon they use it either (a) to put themselves on a level with you, (b) to raise themselves above you, (c) to reduce your level, or (d) to nullify your status (of prestige, authority, knowledge, power, or whatever).

As a consequence, though you must leave talkativeness to others and be a good listener, you must listen aggressively! Which means, you must make listening a weapon and wield it to prevent others from using talking as a weapon.

2. You, not the people themselves, must control how people talk to you

The first big test of yourself as a personal power comes the instant you become a listener. Actually it can be said that whether you go on beyond this point to fully become a self power depends on what you listen to and how you listen.

Because of this, you must immediately develop and begin using listening techniques that enable *you* to control how people talk to you.

3. Use four techniques; the "lend," "fact-finder," "warp" and "servilizor" techniques

There are four basic techniques and each has a definite function: (1) The "lend" technique gives you your listening manner. (2) The "fact-finder" technique wards off those who aim to nullify your status or to put themselves on a level with you. (3) The "warp" technique twists astray those who aim to reduce your level. (4) The "servilizor" technique pushes back those who aim to put themselves above you.

The "lend" technique must be put in operation each and

every time anyone addresses you or begins to talk to you. It must be put in operation the instant you begin your listening and remain in operation every moment that you are a listener.

As to the other three techniques, one or another of them must be exercised each time you listen also, though which is to be exercised is not determinable until the words, tone or manner of the talker discloses how he or she is going to attempt to talk to you! However, immediately this is disclosed, the needed technique must be exercised at once.

To simplify understanding and mastery of the techniques, instead of detailing them beforehand each will be illustrated in its actual application to each of the situations that must be dealt with by you.

4. Listen only as a hearer, never as a hearkener

Except in those instances where a person aimlessly and idly chats with you or merely says "hello," "nice weather," "what'll you have," or the like, the first objective each person has in talking to you is to get your attention, and that is immediately followed by their next objective—to get you to hearken to them!

You should let *every* person accomplish the first objective. You must never let *any* person visibly accomplish the second objective.

That sounds like a harsh statement. Nevertheless, if you are going to get along with people and at the same time build yourself into being a self power, you must master the art of lending your ear to all people and giving it to none.

When any person addresses you or talks to you, you must visibly, wakefully (not preoccupiedly) and attentively hear him, —but use the "lend" technique in doing so.

That means this: You, being the acme of gentlemanliness or ladyliness, extend (as set forth in Chapter 3) respect, courtesy and deference to all who address you. You acknowledge them as individuals, you are gracefully and tactfully considerate of their speaking, and you make due and proper allowance for their having such opinions, knowledge, authority, etc., as they may have. You pay them the compliment of your attention. But that only calls upon you to *hear* them. It does not call upon you to hearken to their words or heed them. In the most literal sense there can be, you lend them your ear, but you do not *give* it to them.

Unless you are gentlemanly or ladylike (as put forth in Chapter 3) you will not be able to exercise the "lend" technique. However, if you are, and your manner visibly is, people will always see you as paying them a compliment by hearing them,—and will not press you to hearken to them.

When the above is true, every conversation is enjoyable. When it is not true (that is, when your "lend" technique is weak), you need to be ready and adept with the other listening techniques.

5. Never let people "hang you on their words"

When people talk to you, their third objective is to hang you on their words. If they can't get you to hang on their *every* word, they try to at least get you to hang on their words as a whole,—or that which they are saying.

They have two aims as they do it. One is to inflate their own importance. The other is to nullify your status or to put themselves on a level with you. Don't let them do it.

If you are competently exercising the "lend" technique, there should be no problem. If you aren't, or if you are tempted (by interest in what is being said) to hang on the speaker's words, you must instantly exercise the "fact-finder" technique: Politely question everything that is said, as it is being said.

For example, inject appropriately: "How do you know that?" "Can you cite a specific instance?" "Who are the 'they' you refer to?" "What is the other side?" Etc.

After the injection of several such questions the person talking to you will abandon the attempt of trying to get you to hang on his words. He will either somewhat abashedly try to slither away from the topic or will present it thenceforth as a more factual report, tendered for your mental perusal rather than for your "swallowing."

6. Never let people gossip to you

Another means people seize upon to put themselves on a level with you is gossip. And if you let them gossip to you, you grant them success. When you listen to a gossiper you bond with him and accept his level. Don't do it.

The "lend" technique alone is never sufficient to prevent a gossiper from gossiping to you. As a consequence, the instant a speaker's tone, manner or words indicate he is set on gossiping, you must exercise the "fact-finder" technique. Again, politely question everything that is said, as it is being said.

For example, inject appropriately: "Where did you hear it?" "Who actually started the rumor?" "What was the purpose?" "Do you believe it?" "Why?" "Why are you telling me?" "Would you expect me to pay attention to it without knowing all the facts?" Etc.

The first three or five questions will usually put the gossiper hopelessly on the defensive and cause him to regret having underestimated you. Most commonly, he will immediately try to reinstate himself with you by "explaining away" his attempt at gossip and by quickly using some other means to court favor with you. You will not have offended him,—instead he will feel guilty of having offended you.

7. Never let people advise you

Still a third means people seize upon to put themselves on a level with you is that of advising you. They may do it by advising you on how to treat a cold, how to change your golf swing, what colors to wear, what stocks to dump, or anything else. No matter what they try to advise you on, and no matter how inconsequential it is, don't let them do it.

No matter who your would-be adviser is, and especially if it is your lawyer, banker, broker, partner, agent, assistant, etc., instantly exercise the "fact-finder" technique. You *must* if you are going on to build yourself into an effective self power.

Again, politely question everything that is said by way of advice, and do so in a manner that will require the would-be advisers to tender to you facts, situations and probabilities instead of advice. Let them include an analysis if they wish to, but let nothing in it be opinion. Use a series of "why's" if need be, but require that they pin everything down to provable facts, definite situations and demonstrable possibilities that will be the basis for *you* making up your mind, not them making it up for you.

8. Never let people apprise you in an informing or instructing manner

As a fourth means of putting themselves on a level with you, and also as a means of even putting themselves above you, people will try to apprise you of things (happenings, bargains, situations, news, etc.) informingly or instructingly. No matter who they are, and no matter what the subject, don't let them do it.

Usually the pattern is something like this: Instead of reportorially recounting something, the person will say, "Did you hear about the new device for so-and-so? It's great. Here's how it works. It—" At that point, and with full politeness, say, "Where did you hear about it?" If the speaker says he read about it (in a newspaper, magazine, etc.), say, "See if you can find me a copy. I'll look it over." If he admits someone told him about it, say, "If you see anything written up on it anywhere, let me know." Often it will turn out that he heard about it only by overhearing a conversation in a restaurant or subway or elsewhere.

This method of pushing apprisers back from their role of self-appointed instructor is a mild form of the "servilizor" technique. In every instance you should exercise it immediately your appriser discloses he intends to take the role of instructor.

9. Never let people "bestow" new knowledge on you

In their attempts to put themselves above you, people frequently will try to bestow knowledge on you instead of imparting it to you. Their success depends on you accepting them as givers of knowledge instead of as communicators of knowledge. Don't do it.

This "bestowal of knowledge" may come from any quarter. However, it poses its biggest threat when it comes from associates, assistants, etc., and particularly if the bestowal is attempted in the presence of others.

The knowledge they try to bestow may be business knowledge, political knowledge, or any other. It may even be knowledge on mechanics, chemistry, or something. Whatever it is, it is something they feel they know and you don't, and they seize upon it to show their superiority.

The words and subject matter may vary slightly, but the bestowal almost always follows either of two patterns. One is the following: You ask a simple question, such as, "Why will our printing costs go up if we change to that cheaper paper?" Instead of giving you a direct answer, the person questioned proceeds to "educate" you on papers, inks, and all manner of things. When this happens, promptly inject, "I thought maybe you knew the answer." The person then will either come forth with a direct answer or will take the defensive and claim he does know and was trying to explain. In either case, you will have pushed him back.

The other pattern is that where, without you asking a question, the person uses a question of his own. For example, the person might take your foregoing question as his own (before you could ask it) and say, "Do you know why our printing

costs will go up if we change to that cheaper paper? I'll tell
you." And then proceed to "educate" you instead of giving the
answer to the question.

Almost anyone might attempt this pattern on you, including strangers. However, the persons who use it most deliberately
on you are those who are about to submit some kind of report
(financial report, sales report, production report, political fore-
cast, or any other). In either instance, promptly inject something such as the following: "If that were written out it might
mean something to me. Do you think it would be worth your
while to write it out for me sometime?"

Again, without offending the person, you've pushed him
back.

10. Use techniques solely to accomplish the things for which the individual techniques are specifically set forth

At this point probably attention should be called to the
fact that, until you are supreme, a liege of no one, some person
or persons may have the right to apprise you instructingly,
"bestow" new knowledge on you, "teach" you, command you,
etc. Such person may be a parent, your landlord, the executive
above you, or anyone else to whom your situation still requires
that you be submissive. In all such instances, so long as you
are "a rung farther down," it would be foolhardy to regard
their exercise of their right as being an attempt at "equalling
or surpassing" your level (which they already are beyond).

The techniques given here (as explained early in the chapter) serve to protect you from persons who would put themselves on a level with you, push themselves above you, pull you
down, or nullify your status. They are not techniques that serve
to pull down those above you (nor are any other self power
techniques). Neither are they techniques meant for use in a
revolt against anyone's proper exercise of acknowledged rights.

On the other hand, they can well be used on any who overstep their rights, and should be, but you yourself must discern what instances may be such (if and when they occur).

In Chapter 19, which concerns itself with "How to Handle Difficult People," the handling of persons who overstep their rights is dealt with, for they (especially those who deliberately try to demean you) are among the most difficult of people and must be dealt with cautiously and through techniques designed especially for the handling of them.

It is pointed out now, however, that the boss who shoots questions at you in order to gain information he can't take the time to find out for himself (or doesn't want to) is not overstepping his rights nor trying to demean you (unless the information deals with things not in the province of your duties). He has assistants, secretaries and other subordinates so that his work load can be distributed (just as you probably do) and his efficiency and effectiveness (like yours) is dependent in great measure on his distributing of his work load and his delegation of duties. And your acceptance of work load and performance of properly assigned duties in no way lowers your level.

Thus, do not use the techniques of this chapter or of Chapter 19 against a boss or other persons merely because you resent their authority or dislike assignments they give you. Use these techniques (and all others) solely to accomplish the things for which the individual techniques are specifically set forth. As you were warned in an earlier chapter, failure to do this can easily cause a technique to boomerang and interfere with your achieving of effective self power.

11. Never let people "teach" you how you should do something

The next problem you face is that of the person who sets out to teach you how you should do something. It may be the man who has just delivered a new TV to you. It may be an employee who wants to "teach" you how to operate some new piece of equipment (instruct you in how to operate it instead ot merely demonstrating how it operates). It may be a stranger who wants to teach you how to cheat a vending machine. On the other hand, it may be an associate or assistant who wants to teach you, not just tell or show you, his way of doing something.

If you weren't building yourself into a personal power you could accept the teaching or could ignore it. As it is though, you can't do either of those. You must push back the attempted display of superiority, no matter how small a one it is.

Here again you need the "servilizor" technique. As the other begins to teach, immediately inject, "There's no use trying to teach me,—just show me how you do it." When he does, immediately say, "Show me again." If he does so, once more say, "Show me again." The next time compliment him. Say, "You're good at it. If I don't know how it's not because you don't know how, is it?"

Most times that will put an end to the teaching attempt. However, if the person tries to resume his teaching, immediately inject, "I'll try it alone sometime. If I have any difficulty I'll call on you."

You've complimented him, but you've pushed him back.

12. Never let people order or command you

There will always be those persons, even a host or hostess, or a fellow traveler or diner, who will be testing their own power and trying to use it to reduce your level. These are the persons who, instead of asking you to do something, tell you to. Some are deliberately rude, some thoughtlessly rude, and others lack such breeding as recognizes rudeness. Regardless of which they be, you can neither ignore them nor obey them,—you must promptly use the "warp" technique and twist their command into a request or appeal or invitation.

When a person issues you a command, even a small one (such as: "Hand me that ashtray."), promptly say, "Did you ask something?"

Unless the person is one who is deliberately being rude, he or she will change tone and manner and say, "Yes. I asked if you would hand me that ashtray."

Where the person is one who is deliberately being rude he or she is likely to instead reply, "Yes. I said to hand me that ashtray." When this happens quietly say, "Sorry. I thought you had asked me something." And then immediately continue the conversation, reading, or whatever you had been engaged in when interrupted.

At this point the rude individual will either (a) apologize and ask for the ashtray; (b) exasperatedly get it himself; (c) say, "Are you or aren't you going to hand me that ashtray?" or (d) repeat his or her command.

Where it is either of these last two that happens, quickly say, "Whomever you are speaking to evidently doesn't hear you. If you care to ask me, maybe I can help."

Only an exceedingly obstinate one-in-a-million will continue to press his command after that. Such a one will repeat the command or double it by telling you, "Stop the foolishness and hand me the ashtray." When this happens promptly say, "If you change your mind and would like me to help you, just ask me." And then again resume whatever you were engaged in, *even if it is conversation with that very person.*

If the foregoing seems to you to be an unnecessary to-do over something, remind yourself of this: You are set upon fully building yourself into being a self power; the closer you approach it, the more will you encounter persons who wish to exert some form of power of their own; you must engage in and win each duel they challenge you with, or else abandon your aims of effective self power.

13. Never let people deliver ultimatums to you

An ultimatum is but another form of command. Like the command, it is used by persons in an attempt to directly exert their own interpretation of power.

No matter what the ultimatum pertains to, use the "warp" technique and deal with it as you deal with a command (and ignore the consequence part of it by which the command was made an ultimatum).

You have but one additional thing to remember: You cannot deal with and dispose of the ultimatum unless you make your ear completely deaf to everything but the command in it.

For example: If your spouse says, "Quit working nights or I'll divorce you!" ignore the "or I'll divorce you" and deal with the "quit working nights" in exactly the same manner as you did with the "hand me that ashtray." That is a simple though extreme example but it is used to point up the fact that if you are to acquire self power you cannot compromise with it (using its techniques on some occasions and not on others), but must fully live by it no matter what the occasion.

Your attention is also called to one more fact that too often is ignored: Except in very rare instances, you yourself have invited the ultimatum by some inconsiderateness on your own part! The day to day ultimatums ("Quit blocking my driveway or I'll—"; "Keep your dog out of my flower beds or I'll—"; "Quit shoving or I'll—"; "If you're late again I'll—"; etc.) are all ones that will not be issued to you if you are observing the prerequisites of self power set forth in the early chapters. If ultimatums of this type occur they occur because you are at fault and your first task is to correct your own faults, not combat the ultimatums.

14. Never let people address you imperiously

The imperious address is likewise but another form of command. The person who says, "You, there," or another such, is trying to exert power.

When you hear a person use an imperious form of address always assume it is meant for some other person and deliberately do not hear it. If the person presses it by accosting you with it or by directly using your name, then immediately exercise the "warp" technique. Deal with it exactly as you deal with a command.

15. Focus on the aim and trick of each technique

The four listening techniques are simple enough. If you put your mind on the aim of each, you will instantly be reminded of the trick it calls for.

The aim of the "lend" technique is to attentively hear without visibly hearkening. The trick of it is to hear another with respect, courtesy and deference while making your manner and reply show that you have taken in nothing of what was said.

The aim of the "fact-finder" technique is to ward off those who try to put themselves on a level with you by getting you to hang on their words or to listen to their gossip or advice or apprisements. The trick of it lies in putting everything they say to question, thereby nullifying the "information value" of the information put forth.

The aim of the "servilizor" technique is to push back those who try to put themselves above you. The trick of it lies in reducing the other person's attempted superiority (of knowledge, etc.) by commissioning him to serve you with it.

The aim of the "warp" technique is to twist astray those who try to reduce your level by exerting power over you. Its trick lies in using a simple question to skillfully maneuver them into requesting or appealing or inviting you to do that which they tried to command you to do.

16. Your "aggressive listening" moves you rapidly toward your goals

Through your aggressive listening techniques you have tightened your grasp on the ball and made great strides in the controlling of people.

Control of others is primarily achieved through controlling their attitudes and thinking by means of your ability to influence these with your manner and word skill.

Every technique given you so far, except the last two, has served to build solely your self power attitude and your manner toward others. The last two ("servilizor" and "warp" techniques) had added to these and have also begun your building of word skill. From here on, all your techniques will deal with word skill as well as your manner.

Your aggressive listening is catapulting you toward the winning, influencing and controlling of others. The techniques that follow are those that secure and protect these as you achieve them.

17. Points worth special attention

1. You must make people reach up toward you (not down) as they talk.

2. Except when in aimless and idle conversation, people all use talking as a weapon.

3. You must listen more skillfully than they talk.

4. Unless you engage in and win each duel you are challenged with you cannot achieve effective self power.

5. Your strongest weapon is that of lending all people your ear while giving it to none.

6. Gentlemanliness or ladyliness must dominate and characterize your listening manner.

7. You must never hang on people's words, and must never allow them to gossip to you, advise you, or apprise you instructingly.

8. With the "fact-finder" technique, you destroy the information value of what they set forth.

9. You must never let people put themselves above you by "bestowing" knowledge on you or "teaching" you.

10. Use the "servilizor" technique to push them back into serving you.

11. The commands, ultimatums and imperiousness of others must never be accepted.

12. Defeat such attempts at exerting power over you by twisting them astray with the "warp" technique.

13. Control of others depends on control of their attitudes and thinking and your primary means of controlling these is your manner and word skill; concentrate more and more strongly on both of these constantly.

9

HOW TO BAG AND POCKET PEOPLE

The people you bag and pocket are the ones you control.
People expect a special voice, words and thoughts from
  you.
The "phone tone" technique leads you into your needed
  talking manner.
Pocketing people requires the professing of thoughts they
  favor.
People look for your talking to have no ring of ordinariness.

So far you've done little talking. In fact, beyond greeting
people and making such remarks as any polite interchange
might call for, you've let others do the talking and you've
confined your own talking to the comments and questions your
listening role has called for. Now you need to punch forth
with some talking of your own,—not talkativeness, just talk,
but the kind of talking that will bag and pocket people.

1. Now that people are intent on you they want you intent on them

Because you have people's attention and interest,—because
you have opened them up to you and pulled friendliness from

78

them,—people in turn want your attention, and through lending them your ear you've given them the first of that attention
they want. Now, however, they want more attention,—they
are intent on you and they want to hear from your own lips
things that will show you are intent on them.

Give it to them. Give it to them solidly, sincerely and straight-
forwardly. Make your manner and words show them *you are*
what they hope you are. Do that, and you will bag and pocket
them effortlessly.

2. The people you bag and pocket are the ones you control

This is the point at which a listener to a lecture on self power
stood up and said, "That's swell. But why do we have to bag
people? Can't we become self powers without it?"

You *don't* have to bag people. You *can* become a self power
without bagging and pocketing people (just as section 8 of
Chapter 3 put forth). *But you can't accomplish your aims unless
you do.* Whatever your aims are, they depend on the controlling
of people, and the people you bag and pocket are the ones
you control!

This you must remember: Self power is but a tool for accomplishing your aims. You can acquire the tool, but to accomplish
your aims you must put the tool to use. Until you put it to use,
self power merely makes you an admired and respected individual, one people bend to and try to please. However, when
you put it to use, exert it to "gather people into your fold,"
or bag them, self power makes everything attainable to you
through those people you thus control.

3. So long as you keep people in your pocket others can't bag them

In your own instance, to achieve your aims, the people you
need most to control may be customers, friends, employees,
stockholders, voters, or any other special group. Whoever they

are, they are .ne people you must be intent on and bag and pocket.

And remember this: You never are the only one interested in controlling those people! No matter who they are, others seek to control them also.

Because of this, you not only need to bag and pocket those people,—you need to keep them there. So long as you can keep people in your pocket, others can't bag them. (Hitler made that truth a fetish. That is why he alone, of all the world's leaders, never feared communism. He bagged the German people and, once he had them pocketed, he focused first and foremost on keeping them pocketed. He made the inducements for them to stay in his pocket ever and ever stronger, so that nothing else could be as rewarding or attractive to them.)

4. It's time to start talking

Because people are intent on you, they expect big and special things from you. The voice, words and thoughts that might satisfy them when coming from an ordinary person are not enough to satisfy them in coming from you. They are intent on you,—that in itself is something special. And they quite rightly expect something special in return.

With your "first inch" technique and your "talk up front" technique, you are already putting your voice out to people in a special way that pleases them. Now you need to add to those with a special talking manner and with special word skill and special thought profession. The people are waiting for those and they are watching you. It's time to start talking.

5. Use the talking manner that people are expecting of you

The first thing people will react to is your manner. They see you as a special person, a self power, and they have seen and heard other self powers before you. In their minds, they associate a definite kind of talking manner with persons of real personal power and, as a consequence, they are looking for your talking manner to be the same.

No matter what talking manner you have had in the past, and no matter what talking manner you may settle upon in the more distant future, for the present you should observe certain techniques that people are expecting of you and will be pleased with.

6. The "phone tone" technique

People are expecting four things of your talking manner,—a definite pitch, a definite speed, a definite sureness, and a definite intensity of delivery. One technique, the "phone tone" technique, can lead you into all of them.

Long before the days of the telephone and the "phone tone" technique the definite pitch needed was described as being a pitch one tone above that which is most commonly used in casual conversation. That description is absolutely accurate but most people are unable, without coaching, to determine when they have their voice pitched at one tone above common casual conversation level. But the telephone has come to the rescue.

With but few exceptions, when people answer a telephone and say "hello" they habitually do so at the very pitch that is the one described. Therefor, unless you are one of the exceptions, all you need do to acquire the needed talking pitch is to pitch your voice at your phone answering tone level!

Practice pitching your voice at that level. A good way to do it is the following. Use the word "hello" to start with (to help you get the pitch) and then work toward multisyllables by saying this series of words and phrases right behind it: "hello," "yes," "no," "maybe," "oh so," "I know," "you know," "lady," "baby," "running," "sliding," "each one," "no one," "hello someone," "in the town," "on the farm," "going around," "merry-go-round," "everyone's merry," "eat, drink and be merry."

After a few tries you should be able to hold the pitch on

through the series and then be ready to use it. And don't be reluctant or negligent in practicing it. Many of the great self powers practice it a minute or two almost every day. One, who is an industrial executive, picks up one phone on his desk and dials the number of his other one,—just so he can answer it and get started off on his practice list with his hello at the perfect pitch!

7. Make your talking speed stay in a range where it can hold maximum interest

The speed at which you talk is as important as your pitch. This because people like to be able to take in whatever you are saying. If you speak too rapidly, they can't, and they lose interest. Likewise, if you speak too slowly or drag your talking, listening to it becomes an effort.

Most self powers try never to let their talking speed go much above 130 words per minute nor much below 110 words per minute. Like public speakers, they clock their rate frequently to make sure they are keeping it within bounds. Some occasionally flick on a tape recorder while they are in conversation so that they can later check exactly how many seconds they used for whatever number of words were in various passages of their conversation.

You yourself can use any method that is convenient to you for establishing and checking your talking speed, but use one that is accurate. Its accuracy is the only thing that is essential, and this because control of your speed depends on it and it is essential that your talking speed be controlled to stay in that range where it can hold maximum interest.

8. Talk only when you know what you intend to say

With your pitch and speed regulated, it is a simple matter to take care of the other two factors of your talking manner.

Definite sureness in your talking manner can always be achieved if you will make it a habit to never start your talking until you know what you are going to say.

That doesn't mean you need to formulate all the words beforehand. What it does mean, however, is that you know what subject you are going to talk about and what you intend to say about it. For example, don't just start talking and then find that your talk has accidentally made a public personality its subject and left you unsure as to whether your comments on him should be favorable or unfavorable.

9. Your intensity should put forth unmistakable sincerity, not heat or pressure

Definite intensity in your talking manner, like speed, is something you must keep within desirable bounds. People don't want you to "sell" them what you are talking about,— they want you merely to put it out fully and clearly in the open. As a result, if you talk too intensely, people are wary. On the other hand, if there isn't at least a shade of intenseness, people feel you yourself are indifferent to and "not sold on" the things you are saying.

The needed intensity may vary but the best definition of what your intensity should at any time be is the following: It should have neither temperature nor pressure; it should be present only enough to be unmistakable sincerity and never enough to be warmth.

10. Profess your thoughts honestly, but only such of them as your hearers will favor

Your thoughts, the "what you say about what you are talking of," always will be heard when your talking manner itself is what it should be.

No one can tell you what your thoughts should be, and even if they should try to, you of course never should allow them. However, when you refer to expressed thoughts instead of inner thoughts, you again find yourself needing to observe bounds.

If you hope to bag and pocket people, a first rule that must guide your thought expression is the following: (a) Never talk on a subject that in any manner offends those who hear you (whether these be the persons you are speaking to or bystanders). (b) Even if the subject is not one that offends hearers, be cautious that what you say about it won't offend them either.

To be more deliberate in your bagging and pocketing of people: (1) talk on subjects that are of their choosing or are ones you know are to their liking. (2) Then, insofar as honesty and forthrightness will permit you to, only say about a subject those things people will like to hear. For example: Should a child of theirs be the chosen subject, talk about her brilliance, her good looks, her lovely hair, and all her other good qualities, but avoid talking about her unmannerliness, her slovenly posture, her questionable companionships, and other bad qualities.

Further: (a) Avoid subjects on which your hearers may be of strongly divided opinions. For instance, avoid the subject of birth control at those times when both devout Catholics and neo-Protestants are among your hearers. Similarly, avoid such subjects as racial ascendency, race disfranchisement, etc., at those times when Boers or Southern Whites and Negroes or Asiatics are among your hearers.

(b) Only talk on controversial subjects when you know your hearers are free of bias. This does not mean that you should avoid controversial subjects. Almost any subject worth talk is a controversial one to someone, and the more talk deals with controversy the greater are its chances of being interesting. However, it not only is a waste of talk to talk regarding a subject on which your hearers have a closed mind, it also turns those hearers against you. For example, it would be indelicate and foolhardy to seize upon the Zionist concept of Israel as a subject when Moslems are among your hearers, and it likewise would be so to seize upon the Christ concept of Jesus of Nazareth as a subject when Jews are among your hearers.

(c) Never use yourself as a subject or an example. Let others do it if they wish, and don't be falsely modest about it, but recognize that for you to do it would lessen the esteem of your hearers. This doesn't mean you shouldn't blow your own horn, for you should. If you can or will do something, state so, but state it positively and as a statement and let it go at that.

(d) Never put opinions forth as opinions,—either put them forth flatly as statements or don't put them forth at all. Anything you put forth as opinion is received as a weakness or uncertainty. If you haven't the knowledge or conviction that would enable you to put a thing forth as a statement you are better off to leave it unsaid.

(e) Never talk apologetically. When you talk apologetically people see you as lacking backbone,—they look on you as a jellyfish that it might be prudent to stay clear of.

(f) Express compliments when you can, but never put forth undue praise or flattery. All people like to be complimented, and all should be complimented whenever they are deserving of it. Such according of due recognition is never taken as courting favor. On the other hand, even those who bask in undue praise and flattery recognize that they are undeserving of the undue praise and look upon your bestowal of it as being either a condescension or a buttering, and in both cases it cheapens you.

(g) Refuse to make a statement rather than let your sincerity in it be open to question. Never say you favor or oppose anything unless you can say it with positiveness, sincerity and reason. Never say you will or won't do something unless you are fully definite. Above all, avoid "maybeing" and its kinfolk.

11. The "thesaurus" technique

Every topic and every situation will call for its own type of word skill (as Chapters 3, 8, 10, 11 and others illustrate). However, your talk itself calls for use of a special word skill that never can be neglected.

The people who are intent upon you don't want you to talk above them and don't want you to talk down. Neither do they want to hear you speak in day to day language. They expect something special of you and they want to hear it. And these things are true whether your hearers are illiterates or literati.

The something special isn't anything you need to concoct or devise. It exists and is available to you, and all you need do is put it to use. The putting of it to use is the special word skill your hearers are expecting of you.

Every person has an interpretive vocabulary that far exceeds that which he uses. In putting expectation upon you, he looks for you to use his interpretive vocabulary, not his day to day one. As a consequence, when you talk he expects to hear you talk in words he understands (ones not above him) but in words that have no ring of ordinariness.

In the main, the words that are in his interpretive vocabulary are in yours also, and the few of those that make up his day to day vocabulary are much the ones that make up yours. Thus, what you need is available to you,—your only job is to pull it into use.

There are various means by which you can select these insufficiently used words and put them to work for you, but one of the best means is to regularly glance through a thesaurus and let it remind you of them and fix them in your mind. In this manner, you build a mental thesaurus of your own,—and gradually you will better and better employ the special words that shade your meanings more specifically toward what it is your intent to say. This, not unusual words, will make your word skill the special something that it's expected to be.

To some extent, your locality, business, etc., will influence the words you most want, and so also will social and economic groups you are among. What is most important is that in drawing on the words you remember that what you want are the generally understood but *insufficiently used* words, not obscure, unusual or seldom seen or heard words.

Any attempted listing of such words would be quite extensive and, for the reasons just given, would include some words that you might not put on your own list while not including others that you would put on your own list. Solely for illustrative purposes, the words that appear on the first page of one such list are given here:

abortive	babbler	cabal	dainty	earnest
abrade	badinage	cache	daunt	ebb
accede	baleful	cackle	dazzle	ebulient
acetous	balustrade	cacophonous	dearth	eccentric
actionable	banterer	cadaver	debacle	ecstasy
admonitory	baroque	cajole	debased	edict
affable	baseness	calamitous	debility	edifice
aggroup	bate	callous	decadence	edifying
aguish	bedaub	callow	decimate	educe
alacrity	beguile	calumny	declaim	efface
allude	berate	canard	decorous	effectuate
allure	bilk	candor	decrepit	effervesce
amatory	bizarre	canny	decry	effete
animus	blabber	capacious	deduce	efficacious
antipathy	bland	caprice	deem	effrontery
apery	blatant	captious	defer	effusive
append	bludgeon	captivating	defile	egregious
apprise	bode	cardinal	delineate	egress
appurtenant	bombastic	caress	delude	ejaculate
archetype	bonhomie	carom	demean	ejection
arduous	boresome	castigate	demoniacal	elate
arrogant	brandish	categorical	demur	elicit
articulate	brashness	caudal	demure	elongate
ascertain	brazen	causative	denote	elude
aspect	brindled	cede	denude	elusory
astute	brusque	celerity	depict	emanate
atrophied	bumptious	censorious	depracatory	embellish
attribute	buncombe	cessation	deter	emblazoned
audacious	buoyant	chameleonic	devious	emergent
auditory	burlesque	chanceful	diaphanous	empirical
augment	burnish	changeful	dilatory	emulation
auspicious	buttress	charlatanism	diligent	enamored
avarice	buxom	chary	discern	enchanting
averse	bye	chaste	disconcert	encroach
awry	byplay	chastise	discrepant	enfeeble

The words shown, though only partially covering those of the first letters of the alphabet, are a good example. Your or anyone s list would include most of them. None of them are unusual or obscure; each of them finds common usage in one field or another; with little exception they are in everyone's interpretive vocabulary; yet, on the whole, they are insufficiently used in most conversation and general talking. By way of further illustration: You yourself might not be able to define all of them accurately at the moment but the chances are good that you would quite correctly interpret each as you saw or heard it used properly in a sentence. Your task is to refresh your mind on the specific implications of these and other such words so that you can be the one to make greater and proper use of them.

12. Points worth special attention

1. People want your manner and words to show them you are what they hope you are.

2. You can't accomplish your aims unless you bag and pocket people.

3. The people you bag and pocket are the ones you control.

4. So long as you keep people in your pocket, others can't bag them.

5. Because people are intent on you they expect special things of you.

6. Talk at a pitch one tone above casual conversation tone; the "phone tone" technique gives it to you.

7. Make your talking speed stay in a range where it can hold maximum interest.

8. Talk only when you know what you are going to say.

9. Make your intensity put forth only unmistakable sincerity, never heat or pressure.

10. To pocket people, put forth only such of your thoughts as they will favor.

11. People expect you to talk in understandable words but words that have no ring of ordinariness.

12. The "thesaurus" technique, not unusual words, makes your word skill the special something it's expected to be.

10

HOW TO BE ON THE OFFENSIVE UNOFFENDINGLY

Once you let another "carry the ball" your self power ceases.

No matter how much you tire, you must never be on the defensive.

Tiredness signals must be heeded instantly.

The "sit on the ball" technique gives you a breather.

Those who challenge you supply your greatest strength.

The befuddler technique defeats those who challenge with inattentiveness.

The dudding technique disposes of the challenging "Why?"

So far you have been concentrating on two aims. You have sought to (1) get along with people, and you have sought to (2) deal with them and present yourself to them in such manner that they want to get along with you. Through the second of these you have been building to a greater self power. Now you must concentrate on one of the main essentials of that self power, —maintaining the offensive!

1. The problem of never being on the defensive

In merely getting along with people, there is no problem of being on the offensive or defensive. As you have already seen, you can be either. In other words, so long as you are pleasant to people, saying and doing things in a manner that pleases them, you "get along" with them. If one of them wants to "carry the ball" instead of letting you carry it, you let him, and thus you "get along" with him. But, as was shown in Chapter 8, such is not the case with self power. Where your self power is at stake, once you let the other person "carry the ball" your self power over him (and all observers) ceases.

Your self power exists only while others see and recognize you as in control of every situation, conversation or action that transpires. Such self features as charm, pleasantness and amiability can be turned off or on and used or displayed at whim but self power must be "on" constantly. Thus, if instead of merely "getting along with people" you are going to exercise self power in dealing with them, you face the problem of at all times maintaining control of every situation, conversation and action in which you participate. This means, *you have the problem of never being on the defensive,*—the problem of "never giving up the ball" to anyone.

2. The problem of maintaining control

When you reflect on it, it's a big problem, isn't it? After all, no matter how much self power you acquire, you are still human. And because you are, it is only natural that from time to time you will tire of constantly maintaining the offensive. And it is this that makes "never giving up the ball" a big problem, isn't it? With that being the case, let's break the problem down, and then lick it in the several ways that are available for doing so.

First of all, take an appraising look at your self power. Focus on that which you do with your self power above and before all else. Put in simple words, *you sell people on yourself,* don't you? You do that first, and then through your accomplishment of that you cause them to perform for you.

Look a little harder at it. You'll see that when you sell people on yourself, you are able to do so because you make them see you as confident, assured, and "carrying the ball" masterfully. Whether you are or aren't those things, you make them see you so. Thus, to keep them sold on you, you must make them see you that way constantly,—and you must do it no matter how much you tire!

It can be done. Your job is to accomplish it, and you have three means for doing it. Skillfully handled, they are techniques for maintaining control.

3. Use of the techniques for maintaining control is essential

Most men never see these three means or techniques as available to them and, as a result, when they tire they either "give up the ball" or they tiredly try to slug their way along. In short, they either drop their offensive or start desperately pushing and jabbing with their offensive and thus offending people with it. You can't afford to do either, for one is as bad as the other. When you "give up the ball" you *discard* control and *abandon* self power. And when you push your offensive, and thus offend people, you antagonize them,—and their antagonism completely blots out any self power you may have had over them.

4. The "sit on the ball" technique

The next time you tire, don't take a chance of being guilty of doing either of those things. Instead, relax, and then just "sit on the ball" for awhile. Do it the very instant anything signals your tiredness. In other words, the instant you tire, quit pushing the offensive but don't let the other fellow take it! Here are some good examples of how you can do it:

(a) One man with a lot of self power is an executive who maintains a heavy nine-hour schedule each day. He says that when he is tiring of "carrying the ball" his tone begins to be crisp and, instead of pleasantly telling or asking people to do things, he begins to order or command them. (Possibly instead of pleasantly saying to his secretary, "See if you can reach Jones for me," he will say crisply, "Get Jones on the phone.") With the first such signal of any tiredness, and regardless of the urgency of any business before him, or of who or how many people he is facing in his office or elsewhere, he instantly and livelily digresses to an entirely dissociated subject that will be certain to interest the person or persons he is talking to, and leads *them* to talk on that subject until his tiredness has passed (whether but a moment or many minutes is required). Then, when his tiredness has passed, he quickly interrupts and "carries the ball onward" from where he had stopped with it.

(b) Another executive, who admits to the same tiredness signals, uses a slightly different method. With the first signal of any tiredness he instantly puts an arguable problem to the person or persons he is talking to, and lets them talk on and wrestle with it until his tiredness has passed. (In one instance the tiredness came on in the midst of lengthily dealing with a three hundred thousand dollar loss; to the other directors he instantly said, "The Internal Revenue Department could be made to shoulder at least half the loss if you would determine what executive salaries to cut, how much and for how long." He had no intention of offsetting the loss in that manner, and he didn't listen to or care about their arguments or estimates; he just wanted to confuse them so he could relax and let them argue among themselves until he was ready to "run with the ball" again.)

(c) Still another executive offers a quite different method. Also, he puts forth one more tiredness signal you can take note of in addition to the more common already mentioned one. He says tiredness causes him to try to ram ideas, opinions and arguments "down the throats" of others. (He is most conscious of this added signal because, during his selling days, failure to heed it was often exceedingly costly.) At the first hint of either of the tiredness signals he instantly puts a diverting question to the person or persons he is talking to, and then relaxes while they try to answer. (On one occasion, when tiredness happened during a session with a particularly difficult female client, he interrupted himself to ask, "Tell me, what is the secret of your easy disposition? Have you cultivated it or were you lucky enough to inherit it?" His manner made it a flattering question and his client couldn't ignore it. When she had spent five or six minutes on attempting an answer to it he was refreshed and ready to "run with the ball" again. And he interrupted her and did so.)

There you have the several variants of the "sit on the ball" technique: (a) Instant and lively digression to a dissociated subject that will be certain to interest the other person and be taken up by him. (b) Instant presentation of an arguable problem that will be taken up by the other person. (c) Instant posing of a diverting question that the other person will feel called upon to answer.

Skill and promptness with the use of the "sit on the ball" technique is absolutely essential to maintaining constant control. It doesn't matter which variant of it you use,—use all of them or which ever one you can adapt to most naturally. Or use a new one of your own invention. But use it the instant you experience a tired-of-the-offensive signal!

As was said in an earlier chapter, every technique depends on some "trick" for its success. The "trick" of the "sit on the ball" technique has three parts and, providing you accomplish them, the means you use to do so aren't important. (1) Remove attention from you and your subject the instant you tire. (2) Relax and keep attention off until your mental vigor is recovered. (3) Bring attention back to you and your subject the instant your mental vigor is regained.

5. Overtiredness of the offensive encourages challengers

Sometimes, because you are so pressing yourself or are so intent on a purpose, you will miss your tiredness signals and others will notice your tiredness of the offensive even before you do. When this happens, it is too late to employ the "sit on the ball" technique so you must be ready and prompt with the second and third of your means or techniques for maintaining control. If you aren't, you will find control has been lost and may even find yourself battling on the defensive.

Everyone who has ever had self power and lost it will warn you that, when others notice your tiredness, they pounce on you.

People are never sympathetic with any tiredness of the offensive. Though you were an idol, or the "boss", or a masterful personality or some other great to them (for minutes or hours or months before), the instant they see you as "tired of the offensive" they jump to the chance of equalizing you or even overstepping you. Don't condemn them for it,—appreciate them, and appreciate and be complimented they are ambitious to be what you already are.

After all, self power is somewhat of a game and you must recognize that the greater yours grows the more susceptible to challenge by others it becomes. Those who offer a challenge to it are your greatest strength while you have it, for their push pushes you on ahead. But, when you fail to exercise it, they equalize or pass you, they don't wait in line behind you. In fact, the only ones left behind you then are "the faithful", the ones who have ridden along on your coat tails to "get somewhere with you" without supplying any of the power for going there. Every once great educator, politician, industrialist, or anyone else who has ever failed to promptly give heed to his tiredness of the offensive, will point these facts out for you as ones to be heeded foremost when one has any real measure of self power.

6. See inattentiveness as a challenge

People have two ways of pouncing on you or challenging your self power when they notice you are tiring and pressing. The first of these may seem harmless, but it isn't, and it can be difficult to overcome. You will find it used against you by employees, associates, customers, and even by people who serve you in restaurants, hotels or anywhere else.

As soon as any of these notice or suspect that you are pressing (with your opinions, ideas, authority, arguments, etc.), your tiredness of the offensive is sensed by them. When this happens, their first and simplest weapon for destroying your offensive (and self power) is to ignore you!

And they do just that. And they do it simply by giving only lackadaisical or unlistening attention to your orders, opinions, commands and wishes.

When you have let your tiredness of the offensive reach that point, what can you do? If you let people get away with their ignoring of you, your control melts away and you are "washed up" as an effective self power. On the other hand, if you fight it by pressing even harder, you either make yourself ludicrous or your manner becomes so offending you make people openly antagonistic. You can't afford to do either of those things, but there is one other thing you *can* do though,—you can verbally throw something at them that they can't ignore. You can fire a befuddler at them!

7. The befuddler technique

The befuddler technique may tax your ingenuity but it is completely effective. Two things are important in the execution of it. First, you must execute it right in stride and without any change of pace or manner. And second, it must never be a threat, but instead must instantly arouse a new interest and curiosity, making use of bewilderment to do so.

Most men with self power have learned two other things about the befuddler technique and are quick to point them out to you. One is to never get in the habit of relying on the befuddler instead of being alert to your tiredness signals (and using the sit-on-the-ball technique). Its effectiveness depends greatly on its rarity, as you will soon appreciate. The other thing they point out is that befuddlers should be prepared in advance against the situations where they may some day be needed. Each situation demands its own type of befuddler and, as a consequence, your own ingenuity must provide and be prepared with the appropriate one whenever you need to fire one. As to this latter, some examples of befuddlers used in different situations will provide you with a few ideas for the devising of your own.

(a) One business owner, well regarded for his self power, relates that he once let his tiredness signals get past him and did not become aware of it until his employees began to ignore him. Obviously he could have forced a greater degree of attentiveness by increasing the assertion of his authority (and thus antagonizing his employees). Instead, he immediately prepared an organization memo instructing every employee to state in five sentences why he or she was an employee of the company and why he or she should be continued as an employee. He gave instructions for a copy of the memo to be given to each employee that day with the replies to be submitted in sealed envelopes before closing time of the following day. And then he disappeared until closing time of the following day.

(b) The president of a small but rapidly growing corporation tells how he did not become aware of his tiredness until he found himself being somewhat ignored in a directors' meeting. He could have pressed for or demanded recognition, but such "power control" of the group would have antagonized his associates. Instead, when the meeting was coming to a close, and with no one suspecting he was referring only to himself, he said, "The value of one member of this board has become questionable to the majority. If the majority feels that that value is still questionable at the date of our next meeting, I'll expect to hear a proposal of resignation offered."

(c) A salesman with a lot of personal power tells how he failed to heed his tiredness signals and suddenly found an important customer was totally ignoring his sales effort. He could have pressed for attention and chanced antagonizing the customer, but he didn't. Instead, without changing his tone or manner, he said, "If you are anticipating an income decrease, you're wise to not buy until you have to, because your low income dollar will have a higher purchasing power. However, if there is a likelihood of your income increasing, your present income dollar is your low income dollar and already has a far higher purchasing power than your tomorrow's dollar will have and therefor what you buy today will cost you considerably less."

(d) A politician of considerable self power tells of how he once let his tiredness signals slip past him and as a result found a large audience restless, rather inattentive, and some even ignoring him and talking between themselves. He could have rapped for order, shouted louder, or done other things, none of which would have been to his advantage. Instead, without changing his manner or interrupting his arm waving and table thumping, he suddenly made his mouth form every word *without issuing any sound* and thus continued on with his speech in animated silence. Within a few seconds every eye was fastened on him and there was total silence. And then, with still no change of manner, he let the words again come aloud from his mouth and gave no indication that he was aware of the period when they hadn't!

There are many dozens of interesting examples of the befuddler technique that could be recounted. All of them however, no matter how different they are, have the same qualities: Each suddenly induces bewilderment that gives birth to a curious and renewed interest. Further, almost none are spontaneous. They are cautiously devised and well planned far in advance.

As just one illustration of this planning, the politician mentioned was highly conscious of the fragileness of all self power. A half dozen years prior to having to use his befuddler, he devised what befuddler he *would* use if his tiredness signals ever got past him while addressing an audience!

You too may at any time miss your tiredness signals. You should plan now against its happening and have at least one befuddler ready for each of the several situations where you ever may need to use one (employees, associates, a customer, an audience, or any other in your sphere). But, with or without a befuddler ready, you should try to assure that the situation never occurs. In other words, recognize that it *can* occur and be prepared, but do your utmost to remain alert to your tiredness signals so that it *won't* occur. If you have ever seen even a little "self power" fail in such a situation (and you must have witnessed at least one or more), you know how permanently damaging and pitiable such a failure can be!

The trick of the befuddler technique can be reduced to a few words: The instant another or others ignore you, say or do something that will bewilder them.

8. A challenging "Why?" is ominous

The second of the ways by which others challenge your self power is a direct opposite of the ignoring of you. And when they use it on you, you will know you have let your tiredness of the offensive reach the bottom point. People only use it when they *know* you have lost your assurance and are overpressing. Thus, they use it only when they believe that their use of it will force you to abandon the offensive and become defensive!

From childhood on, you (and all people) seem to inherently know that you can force another to become defensive by simply firing "Why?" at him challengingly. You have done it. And you have had others do it to you. But, others never do it to you after you acquire self power unless they see your offensive as weakening and vulnerable.

If you badly overpress with associates or employees—or even on a sale or with friends—you are bound to offend or antagonize, and when you do, a "Why?" will challenge you. Sometimes the challenge will be made with a sentence that emphasizes the "Why?" but, most often, the challenge will be nothing more than that one word alone, put forth in a manner that charges, "Prove you know what you're talking about." When it happens, *you don't dare answer it,* for answering *or even attempting to answer* is abandonment of the offensive. And you don't dare "bat it back," because to do so acknowledges vulnerability

You should always be able to distinguish a challenging "Why?" from a genuine information seeking one. If you can't, or if you are ever in doubt, the safest course is to treat every "Why?" as a challenge!

9. The dudding technique

Though you don't dare answer the "Why?" or bat it back (or let it irritate you in any manner), neither do you dare walk away from it. Instead of doing any of those, if you are to hold and restrengthen your offensive (without offending or antagonizing) you must instantly put forth or pose a diverting or distractive question. And then quickly add or follow-up with a second question that will return your challenger to the defensive.

When you do exactly that, you turn your challenger's "Why?" into a dud and make a boomerang of it without antagonizing him,—and he readily drops the challenge of your offensive power.

The questions you use for dudding your challenger's "Why?" must be strictly diverting or distractive! And must never be made as a counter challenge. If you make them as a counter challenge you either reduce yourself to "crossing swords" with the challenger or you show yourself as evasive (and thus as being as vulnerable as he thought you were). As with befuddlers, there are no pretailored dudding questions, but here again are some examples that can guide you in the devising of your own:

(a) A challenging "Why?" (in response to announcement of a new sales policy) awakened a sales manager to his tiredness. His first inclination was to yell, "Because I said so," but he instead said, "I'm glad you opened the subject. I've been wondering why you didn't give your wife those jade earrings she wanted for her birthday. She had her heart set on them and they wouldn't have cost you any more than what you did give her, would they?"

(b) A freight line executive became aware of his tiredness when one of his warehouse superintendents fired a challenging "Why?" at him (with regard to catching up a backlog without using overtime). He held back a retort of, "Because your own inefficiency caused it," and instead said, "That reminds me. I've been wondering why we don't use women to operate the forklifts. Wouldn't they cut costs by wasting less time and being more careful with the loads?"

(c) A board chairman was warned of his tiredness when a junior director threw a challenging "Why?" back at him (regarding jurisdictional changes). Refraining from pointing out that the junior director had too often shown a lack of maturity in judgement, he said, "I asked myself that question beforehand and it led me to another. Wonder how many of our supervisory and executive personnel are conscious that, as such, they must function in the triple role of employee, employer, and subcontractor? Wouldn't it be a good idea to appraise everyone from top to bottom and cull out any who aren't competent in or fully attentive to all three of their roles?"

Those examples let you see how the dudding technique is practiced and why it is effective. The "Why?" is not ignored, is not answered, and is not batted back. In each instance it is treated as a lead to another subject, and the questions used are such as will cause the challenger to deliberate whether they are a subtle reply. Invariably, the challenger will decide there is some connection and that it might have been better not to make the challenge! As a consequence, instead of furthering his antagonism, you have quelled it and regained his respect.

10. Maintaining permanent control and self power

As said at the beginning of this chapter, if you are to have effective self power you at all times must maintain control of every situation, conversation and action in which you participate, and you can only maintain that control by constantly being on the offensive *and being on it unoffendingly*. Previous chapters have given you the techniques for getting along with people and winning them to you as you take and build the offensive. This chapter has given you the techniques for keeping people won over despite the human failings you and all of us are subject to. If you heed your tiredness signals, and use these three techniques promptly, your exercise of self power will never offend or antagonize anyone and you will always maintain control of them.

11. Points worth special attention

1. Keep your self power turned on constantly.
2. Never "give up the ball" to anyone.
3. Never risk offending or antagonizing others.
4. If you feel yourself tiring of the offensive, use the "sit on the ball" technique.
5. Remove attention from you and your subject the instant you tire.
6. Relax and keep attention off until your mental vigor is recovered.
7. Bring attention back to you and vour subject the instant your mental vigor is regained.
8. If you overtire (so that others ignore you) use the befuddler technique.
9. Say or do something that will bewilder others the instant they ignore you.
10. If your tiredness puts vour offensive at bottom and others challenge you, use the dudding tecnnique.
11. When a challenging "Why?" is thrown at vou, treat it as a lead to another subject.
12. Pose a distractive question instantly.

11

HOW TO STRENGTHEN YOUR INDIVIDUALITY

A self power must be an archetype and a source to be adequately individual.

Unconscious mannerisms of actions and speech are a part of your individuality.

Your individuality is strengthened when you speak only your own mind and show yourself a source.

The "me-tooism" excluder technique makes your thoughts assertive and also eliminates "crutch" thoughts.

The "quote quash" technique rescues you from the self quoting error.

The source technique eliminates the quoting of others and makes you speak your own mind.

You have made people see you and notice you as a definite and distinctively individual being. More specifically, you have made them conscious of your physical self (that which they see) as being distinctively individual. And then, through your manner of speaking, you have indicated that your mental self may be distinctively individual also. Now you must demonstrate a mental individuality, make your individuality be heard as well as seen.

1. You must be a source, not an interpreter or amplifier of one

The greater your power becomes, the more it and you are subjected to scrutiny. You have been reminded of that before and you will be reminded of it again. It is a thing you must henceforth be increasingly aware of and constantly heed. Each increase of your self power means added eyes and ears noticing everything you do and say. And the more of them that notice you, the more critically are you seen and heard by some among them.

You already have been given techniques and admonishments on your talking manner and choice of subjects. Those things get you on your way and initiate your control. Now you must make people see your actions and your mind as your own, see both as being as distinctively individual as all else about you. Said more bluntly, you must make people see you as a genuine self, an archetype, not as a copy of someone else nor as a mere imitator of others or as a rephraser or voicer of others' thinking. *You must be a source,* not an aper, interpreter or amplifier of what some other source offers.

2. Your natural mannerisms give you individuality so long as they do not intrude on your consciousness

It is very doubtful that people themselves are conscious of how closely they scrutinize you. Nevertheless, there is little if anything about you that they miss. They take in everything, —your mannerisms, your speech peculiarities, your quoting, your repetitions, and all the rest.

Your visible mannerisms quite naturally get first attention, but so long as they are your own you have nothing to worry about. Like the self power attitude, they catch eyes and, if they are your own, they are seen as a part of you, as making up your individuality.

You, like all of us, have many mannerisms you aren't aware

of in addition to the other few that are well known to you. Some are facial mannerisms, others are postural, and others are things you unconsciously, maybe reflexly, do with your hands or shoulders or other parts of your body. (For example: It isn't likely that one top executive realizes that whenever he thinks intensely he swallows successively and wiggles his ears. And neither is it likely that a quite prominent politician realizes that his scalp moves back and forth and lets his opponents know whenever he is discomposed!)

No matter what your visible mannerisms may be, ignore the ones you don't know about and never even try to learn of them. Since they are a part of you that contributes to your individuality you shouldn't meddle with them or let yourself become conscious of them. The worst they can be is amusing or distractive, and those qualities won't cause mannerisms to interfere with your self power. Assure yourself that if the unknowns were serious mannerisms (offensive, repulsive, etc.) you most certainly would have had your attention called to them before now.

As to such mannerisms as you have and are aware of (if any), try to wipe them from your consciousness. In any event, don't promote them; if you can't wipe them from your consciousness, either successfully ignore them or get rid of them. Above all, don't do anything that will make you self-conscious because of them. Again, when you are unconscious of them they are a part of what gives you individuality and the more you can let them alone the more of individuality you'll have. However, if they intrude on your consciousness you *can't* let them alone, so for that reason it is still best to rid yourself of them if you can't ignore them.

3. Affected mannerisms of action or speech destroy your individuality

Right here is where you need to be cautious on another score: Do *not* let yourself fake, take on, acquire or use any invented or borrowed or copied mannerisms. Time and again persons climbing toward self power affect mannerisms, often copying those of some established self power. Whenever you do this, two things happen and work against you. First, the mannerisms always manage to show themselves as affectations; as copied instead of natural. Second, observers are quick to spot the apery and, when they do, they look upon the whole of you as but an apery,—they see and regard you as a pretender to self power instead of as a genuine self power.

These and the other things said about mannerisms apply not only to your visible mannerisms (your actions, etc.) but also to your audible mannerisms, your mannerisms of speech, voice, pronunciation, and the like. For example, if you copied the Dwight D. Eisenhower word stumbling mannerism, the Franklin D. Roosevelt phrase overpitch monotoning, or the Alfred E. Smith emphasis of syllabic unconventionalities, how much individuality could those give to you? None, of course. Instead your copying of them would blot and blur whatever true individuality you now have.

No matter what the temptations, no matter how much some mannerism (visible or audible) seems to work toward the benefit of some other person or self power, never let yourself take it on. Make sure you never have these nor any other mannerisms that you need be conscious of. As already said, any mannerism that intrudes on your consciousness never shows itself as a natural part of you. On the other hand, those that do not impose themselves on your consciousness genuinely are a natural part of you, and thus strengthen your individuality and contribute to the genuineness of your self power.

4. Whether or not you are a thought power, your thoughts will wield power if you are a thought source

A common failing of many would-be powers is that of striving to be a so-called thought power, an utterer of profound thoughts.

One of the most pitiable examples of this mistake is a well pub-
licized Senator who has made himself ludicrous to all his
colleagues and the members of the press by his constant attempts at intoning every little thing as a profound thought.
You don't need to be a Confucius for your thoughts to wield
power,—all you need to do is demonstrate that you have the
ability and courage to think and speak thoughts that are your
own.

People are not looking for or expecting your thoughts to be
profound,—they are only looking for them to be original. As
was already mentioned, because you show as a self power
people also expect you to be a source of thought. When you
have a self power attitude, and exercise it and your self power
techniques to interest and draw people, people expect your
thinking to be your own and in keeping with those facets of
you. Thus, it too must have an instantly apparent distinctive
individuality!

Here again the strength of your individuality depends some
on what you do but mostly on what you avoid doing. The
general rule is: (1) Speak only your mind, not someone else's;
(2) avoid quoting; (3) never quote yourself *except in emphasis prior to reassertion;* and (4) never quote anything of another unless it is something you *of necessity are going to
pointedly contradict or refute,* and then quote it only introductory to the contradiction or refutation.

At first glance that rule and its admonishments may seem
unnecessary; you may think you already speak your own mind
and that therefor its admonishments don't apply to you. However, if you will examine it, *and yourself,* more closely, you
will quickly recognize that neither you nor any of us commonly speak our minds in the sense put forth. As you follow
through and delve into it you will see why even the greatest of
self powers often have difficulty adhering to that rule, important as they know it to be.

The importance of that rule boils down to this: People do

not overly expect or demand that you (or any self power) be a thought power, but they do expect you to be a thought source, a speaker of original thoughts. Thus, if you always show your thoughts as your own, your thoughts wield power whether you yourself are a thought power or not!

5. Eliminate "me-tooism" first of all

The first item in the rule just given is the matter of speaking only your own mind, not someone else's. This refers to thoughts and thoughts only. Even so, how often have you said, "Howard thinks the price is too high and I'm inclined to agree with him."; or, "Jones prefers to travel by train and so do I."; or, "Isabelle suggests we should start at eight-thirty and I subscribe to the idea."; etc.?

In every such instance, instead of speaking your own mind you have spoken a thought as someone else's and have merely shown yours as being in harmony. Whenever you have done so, instead of asserting your individuality *you have engaged in a form of "me-tooism"!* You must not do it! Reversely, you instead must speak the thoughts as yours, and then show, if need be, that the other's thought is but one in harmony with yours!

When going through a door with others, when taking food or refreshment with them, or when naming them conjunctively with yourself (the gift was from Jim, Ed and me) it may be polite and conventional to "put others first," but, where thoughts are concerned, unless you put yourself first (destroy all "me-tooism") you quash your self power. From here on you must use the "me-tooism" excluder technique everytime you express a thought. You must put yourself first in every instance.

6. The "me-tooism" excluder technique

The "me-tooism" excluder technique has two jobs. First it must eliminate all your "me-tooism" habits, and then it must kill your crutch thoughts habit.

For example: Using the "me-tooism" excluder technique on

the statements made several paragraphs earlier, say, "I think the price is too high; Howard does also." But, do *not* say, "and Howard agrees with me," or any like thing; it would cause your hearer to feel you lacked confidence or conviction in your thought and that you were using Howard as a crutch for it.

As those examples well demonstrate, when you put forth your own thought first, and then merely courteously or informingly append another's thought to it, your thought stands alone, on "its own feet" so to speak. But, when you deviate from this any particle, that is, put forth that thought of the other as one with or in conjunction with yours, your thought does not stand alone; it uses the thought of the other as a supporting thought. You dare not let that happen. As a self power, you must at all times show your thinking as standing alone, just as you show yourself as standing alone.

7. Heed the trick of the technique and you'll avoid both "me-tooism" and crutch thinking

Ridding yourself of "me-tooism" and crutch thinking isn't difficult. To the contrary, there is a danger you may try to go too far with it (apply it where it doesn't apply). To guard against this, never try to apply the technique to anything that isn't including some thought of your own. By way of illustration, a statement such as, "Jones thinks he's lost the client," has no "me-tooism" or crutch thinking in it (since it contains no opinion or thought of your own). Let it stand as a flat statement, because any attempt at applying the technique to it would necessitate injecting your thinking.

Your best approach to speaking your own mind is a simple one and has only two parts. Observe it fully at all times and your thoughts will always stand "on their own feet" and give extra strength to your individuality. Put simply, it is this: Regardless of what the subject and how casual the conversation, put your thinking forth *only in the form of a statement*. Do not mention another's thinking unless you need to and, if you do, state *your* thinking first and then *(merely courteously or informingly, never supportingly)* show that of the other as being in addition to your thinking, not as with yours or in conjunction with it.

That procedure for speaking your own mind is really the whole of your "me-tooism" excluder technique. It makes the technique simple and effective and you'll have no trouble with it if you will heed the trick of it, which lies in (1) always stating your thinking first and (2) *never* following your thinking with "and," "as," or any other connective word.

As an added tip: If you will make it habit to state your thinking first, and then to *state it briefly and quickly clip it,* you'll soon acquire the knack of avoiding "me-tooism" and crutch thinking.

8. Quoting is rarely necessary and almost always detracting

The next item in the rule for speaking your own mind is the matter of avoiding quoting.

Quoting very rarely has any merit. You have time and again heard it referred to as a "sign of weakness," as resulting from "lack of conviction," or as bespeaking "no self-confidence. Though it rarely has merit and very often is those things, it must be conceded that there are times when it isn't. However, even when it isn't, and even when it has merit, it most certainly is more often done from habit than from necessity. This applies as much to the quoting of yourself as it does to the quoting of others.

To prove to yourself that these things are true, read the drafts of some of your speeches. If none of these are available read the reprints of other persons' speeches (whether these were delivered on political subjects, scientific subjects, business subjects, or any other) and circle all the quotes you come across.

When you finish, go back and inspect each one. You will find that very few (or maybe none!) of the quotes was necessary; almost all were used as crutches or as inflaters.

What is true of the quotes in your speeches is even more true of the quotes in your business talking, sales talking, informal talking and casual conversation. In general it more often than not fails its purpose and, because it mostly is unnecessary, it almost always is detracting.

9. Never let self quotes show you as "importance" seeking

The third item in the rule for speaking your own mind is that of never quoting yourself except in emphasis prior to reassertion.

Consider first the times you quote yourself carelessly or in offhand remarks. Are you aware of how frequently you do so? Often you make such remarks as, "I said that a week ago."; or, "I warned three months ago the market would tighten."; or, "I said he wouldn't last long."; etc.

Though those are seemingly harmless and strictly "conversational" quotes of yourself, all such quotes make your hearers look upon you as seeking to gain a self importance that you are afraid they don't see you as having. And, whether you heretofore or not have realized it, that's exactly what such self quotes are!

So that your quoting of yourself won't be that and will never destroy your projection of self power, adhere strictly to the rule and never quote yourself *except in emphasis* of a definite and strong assertion that the quote is to introduce!

Though even this type of self quoting should be held to a minimum, here are some examples of it: "I said a week ago the public will react strongly; I say it again, the public will react strongly and our sales will skyrocket." And, "I warned three months ago the market would tighten; it has, and I warn that it will tighten even more." Also, "I said he wouldn't last long; events now show he won't and can't last long."

10. The "quote quash" technique

The "quote quash" technique involved in your avoidance of self quoting is a simple one. It calls but for two things: The first is, don't let yourself make self quotes (clamp your lips, bite your tongue, or do whatever else it takes to stop yourself whenever you start to make a self quote). The second is, if through a slip of the tongue you *do* make a self quote, instantly kill it as a quote by treating it as an introductory statement and following it immediately with a definite and strong assertion that furthers it!

Make it habit to adhere to this procedure every time you speak, talk or converse. If you are alert you'll have no trouble with it. (And as the preceding chapter pointed out, to maintain your self power you must never talk or converse unless you are alert).

When a self quote slips by you, even a supposedly unimportant one, such as, "I said yesterday it would rain today," kill it as a quote at once. Treat it as an introductory statement and immediately append something to it. For example! "and to make sure it would I had my car washed." Or, "because that barometer I got for Christmas hasn't been wrong yet." Say those or anything else that comes to mind. The most important thing is that you append something, *anything*, that will seriously, jokingly or otherwise turn the quote into an introductory statement and quash it as a self quote.

Heeding the first suggestion of the "quote quash" technique will quickly reduce your habit of self quoting. Heeding the second one will both rescue you from your errors and make your intential self quotes undamaging. Observe the second one in every instance of self quoting (both intentional and accidental quoting) and your hearers will never look upon your self quote as a "self" inflater.

11. Never engage in the quoting of others when it is in any way avoidable

The fourth item in the rule for speaking your own mind is the matter of never quoting another unless it is something you of necessity are going to pointedly contradict or refute.

Despite the harm that self quoting can do to your projection of self power, the quoting of others can be even more harmful. Shun it; never traffic in it, and touch it only when you are forced to! In other words, never engage in it when it is in any way avoidable. And see it as always avoidable except in those instances where a pointed contradiction or refutation is called for *and necessary!*

Emphasis is put on the "and necessary" because, other than in those instances where a situation actually demands a contradiction or refutation, your bothering to contradict or refute a thing serves to enhance it, give it added importance,—and at the same time serves to lessen your own stature.

12. Never bother to contradict or refute a falsity or error unless attack on it is necessary

As you well know, whenever you contradict or refute anything another has said you always directly or indirectly quote it. Thus, if you are to avoid quoting others, you must avoid making contradictions or refutations except where they are absolutely necessary.

Actually, contradictions and refutations very rarely are necessary. The mere fact of something being erroneous, false or untrue and you knowing better is not a sufficient one to make a contradiction or refutation of it necessary.

To best illustrate this, let's take an extreme: If someone says, "You're a charlatan," your bothering to refute it establishes— in the minds of others—that whether or not the statement is true there are grounds for it. As a consequence, no matter how completely and thoroughly you verbally refute the statement, you end up with less stature than if you had ignored it (treating it as one too ridiculous and obviously false to be worthy of even acknowledging it as heard let alone worthy of refute).

The same is applicable to less extreme things. In general, the less extreme or smaller a falsity or error is, the smaller you make yourself when you bother to contradict or refute it!

For example, statements like "the bus was about a half hour late" or "hundreds of people were there" may be known to you to be false. However, your knowing that the bus was only "ten minutes late" and that only a "few dozen people were there" does not make contradiction of those other statements necessary. As a result, if you do contradict such statements when another makes them you show yourself as smally troubling to belittle him.

To the reverse however, if rival interests among the stockholders are falsely saying (in an attempt to overthrow you) that the company has lost money under your leadership, the situation easily could demand a refutation, particularly if the rival interests are going so far as to distort what the financial statement shows.

In such an instance (and for the reasons given) you still must refrain from ordinary contradiction or refutation. In addition, simple refutation would be insufficient anyway because it would be accepted only in the light of a defense. Therefor, the called for refutation must be introduced by definitely quoting the false charge *and then attacking it*. Emphatically, your refutation must be *an attack* on the false charge, *not a defense* against it. This is not because "attack is the strongest defense"; it is because, as stressed in Chapter 10 and elsewhere, you as a self power must constantly maintain the offensive, never be defensive!

The rule then is, unless *attack* upon an error or falsity *is necessary*, never bother to contradict or refute it.

13. When you quote another you add to his power and deplete your own

Allowing but for the one exception just covered, always avoid quoting anything whatever of another. Some of the reasons for this have already been given and the others should be evident to you. If they aren't, you can easily measure them by what your own reactions are when you hear someone else quote another. Let's list them separately so that the damaging strength of each will stand out for you:

First, the fact that you quote another indicates to your critical hearers that you believe the words of the other will wield more power and influence with them than your own would.

Second, it indicates to your hearers that you consider that what is quoted is more important because the other said it than it would be if you said it.

Third, it shows you as being reluctant to accept responsibility for saying it, as unwilling to meet any challenge of it, and thus as ducking and putting the responsibility for it on the other.

Fourth, it shows you as ranking yourself and your own thoughts on a lower level than you rank the other and his thoughts.

Fifth, it shows you as lacking the strength to be an individual; as being only a voicer or amplifier for the other's thoughts, and not a source of independent and distinctively individual thought (the thing a self power *must* be).

Obviously, if you are to assert and maintain self power you must never let yourself be looked upon in any of those ways. You must always be seen as a source (as emphasized in section 4 of this chapter), and most certainly you cannot be looked upon as a source when you quote others as being your source. Here, as in the already covered instances of speaking your own mind, you must either relegate the thoughts of others to secondary status or eliminate them entirely. No matter how bad a quote addict you are, you must break the quote habit. The source technique will help you do it.

14. The source technique

To break yourself of the quote habit and make yourself the source you must be, never speak or talk, even in casual conversation, without using the source technique and making it govern every statement and thought you put forth. Unlike the other techniques for speaking your own mind, the source technique isn't a speaking trick or word trick, it is basically a resolve.

Your first move in employment of the source technique is your most difficult one. It slows you down. It requires that, before you attribute any statement to another, no matter how insignificant it may seem, you examine it. Further, it requires that you make this apply to offhand and shunt remarks as much as to profound statements.

With regard to shunt remarks, all day long you hear (and maybe make) such opening statements as, "They say —", "Everyone says—", "It's reported that —", "I hear —", "They tell me—", etc. When you are a self power, the making of such shunt quotes is even more damaging to you than the making of direct quotes. Shunt quotes damage you in the same five ways as do direct quotes and in one additional one: They show you as an unspecific and careless quoter, the kind who (innocently or otherwise) starts rumors!

15. Weigh whether you yourself know, believe, feel or accept what you are about to quote

The first requirement of the source technique, as said, is that before you attribute any statement to another (directly or indirectly, specifically or indefinitely) you examine it. When you do this, don't just "look" at the statement. Weigh it. Ask yourself (a) whether it is a fact you yourself know, (b) whether it is a thing (eventuality, etc.) you yourself believe, (c) whether it is something (reaction, emotion, etc.) you yourself feel, or (d) whether it is a thing (condition, theory, etc.) you yourself accept.

Don't treat this weighing of statements in this manner lightly. It's the foundation of your source technique and there is little chance that you'll ever make yourself a source unless you engage in it. On the other hand, when you do engage in it you'll quickly see how foolish much of your past quoting has been.

16. Drop the rejects; don't hand over the ball

In some instances your examination will show the fact or thing *not* to be any of the foregoing (a, b, c or d). When such is the case, investigate it further if you wish to, but do *not* give voice to it. Reject it! In every instance of this kind, rejection specifically means "refuse to quote it" and refrain even from commenting on it. Thus, deny it notice of any kind!

There is, of course, also the possibility that your examination will disclose that the fact or thing is the *opposite* of what you know, believe, feel or accept. Where this is the case, you here too should deny it notice of any kind. Only one exception to this exists and it was mentioned in section 12 of this chapter: When, because of what the fact or thing is attendant to, contradiction or refutation of it is called for *and necessary*, it must not be ignored (and again emphasis is put on the "and necessary"); it must instead be attacked.

In connection with the mentioning of attack at this point it should be stressed that the tactics of questioning, voicing doubt, challenging for substantiation, etc., do not constitute an actual direct attack and none of these should be employed (in such an instance or any other). The reason: Employment of these (a) shows you yourself as being an indecisive person, (b) shows you as being too weak to counter, and (c) gives the other person the upper hand. Each of the tactics spurs the other to greater assertiveness and positiveness, affords him attention, adds to his strength, and yet offers no opposition. In effect, it "hands him the ball" and gives him a clear field! As emphasized in Chapter 10, to be an effective self power, you must never give up the ball to anyone! Thus, (and allowing for but the one stated exception) no matter how negative a fact or thing is to what you know, believe, feel or accept, totally deny it notice.

17. The source technique merely makes you do what you all along should have done

With the negative possibilities disposed of, the remaining possibility is that of your examination showing that the fact or thing is one you know, believe, feel or accept. When this happens, your second move in employment of your source technique is to put the fact or thing into your own words and speak directly of it as a thing *you* know, (or believe, feel or accept), not as something some other does.

To be effective as a self power you must reason this way: Since you yourself do know, believe, feel or accept the fact or thing you have no excuse for attributing it to another. Therefor, if you were to attribute it to another instead of to yourself, you would be showing weakness and timorousness; you would be deficient as a self power. Opposed to this, when you on the other hand attribute it to yourself and thus accept full responsibility for it, you show yourself a source,—you strengthen your individuality.

In the regular sense, there is no trick to the source technique. Its trick, if it has one, is that of making you do something you all along should have done.

With all the explanations and illustrations stripped from it, the procedure of the source technique is as follows: Resist the temptation to quote; if you can't resist, examine and weigh every fact or thing before you quote it; if it is not one you yourself know, believe, feel or accept, reject it; if it is one you yourself know, believe, feel or accept, don't quote it as something put forth by another,—take full responsibility for it by putting it in your own words and attributing it to yourself. Unless you are willing to do that, you have no business saying it at all.

This source technique, or what it does for you, is probably the biggest single factor in the strengthening of your individuality. In addition, it is the foundation for your projecting of individualism. As such it takes on added importance. Specifically, if you abide by it fully and never deviate, it will merge with the steps in the chapter that follows and will enable you to project a degree of individualism that is rare even among prominent self powers.

18. Points worth special attention

1. You must aim at being an archetype.

2. Rid yourself of conscious mannerisms but ignore any that don't intrude on your consciousness.

3. Show your thoughts as your own and they'll wield power whether you yourself are a thought power or not.

4. Eliminate all your "me-tooism" habits.

5. Use the "me-tooism" excluder technique to make your thoughts "stand on their own feet" and to free them of crutch thoughts.

6. Avoid quoting; quoting rarely has merit and is almost always unnecessary.

7. Self quoting destroys the self power image; it makes others see you as "begging" importance.

8. Use the "quote quash" technique to destroy your self quoting habits and to rescue you from your errors.

9. Never quote others unless it's unavoidable; it's always avoidable except where a refutation is absolutely necessary.

10. When a refutation is necessary, attack with it; never take the defensive.

11. Quoting another adds to his importance and reduces yours; it shows you as weak, ducking responsibility, and downgrading yourself.

12. You must relegate the thoughts of others to secondary status or eliminate them entirely.

13. Use the source technique to cure yourself of the quote habit.

14. Shunt quotes are the most damaging of all; they show you as an unspecific and careless quoter, the kind who starts rumors.

15. Never use the tactics of questioning, voicing doubt, etc.; they make you appear weak and indecisive and they "hand the ball" to the other person.

16. If a fact or thing is something you yourself know, believe, feel or accept, you have no excuse for attributing it to another; put it into your own words and take full responsibility for it; unless you're willing to do that, you have no business saying it at all.

12

HOW TO PROJECT INDIVIDUALISM

Your individuality comes alive when you talk, speak and converse from an ever-changing inventory of phrases and material.

Supplanting conventional greetings and responses with ones having an interest-arousing characteristic is a must.

The "topic teaser" technique gives your openings newness and life.

The body or text of what you say needs to have a living individuality also.

When alternates displace ill-used, abused and set phrases your talk acquires a new and distinctive quality.

The tidbit technique makes you a distinctively individual, interesting and non-routine conversationalist.

Now that you are making people both see and hear you as an individual you must push on with your individuality and make it a more living thing. You have made your thoughts "stand on their own feet" but that isn't enough; you need to make them themselves bespeak an individuality too. When you can make them do that, you'll project a true and unmistakable individualism.

1. A fluid inventory of phrases and material, used in talking, speaking and conversing, can project individualism for you

Everything about you that is of a distinctively individual character contributes to your individuality, and so far you've built a lot of it. When you take that individuality and put life into it, translate it into independent and singular initiative, action and interest, you take on a new and even more individual quality. It is this quality that is referred to as individualism. With what you now have of individuality, you will easily be able to develop and project individualism of a kind that will be favorable and impressive, and add measurably to the self power image you already are projecting.

There are many means of projecting individualism but only one of them is effective on all people (and accepted and given understanding by all). The one favorable means of projecting an effective individualism is that of talking, speaking and conversing from an ever changing inventory of phrases and material.

There are two ways in which you can make a fluid inventory of phrases and material project individualism for you. One focuses on greetings and opening remarks and the other focuses on your running talk or the text material of speeches and conversation. Let's take them in that order.

2. Conventional greetings and responses are devoid of individuality

Immediately you focus on greetings and opening remarks you are awakened to how routine they are,—and to the realization that any supplanting of their stock phrases is sure to project some individualism. The eliminating of all those stock phrases and customary material from your greetings, opening remarks, initial responses, and other of your first words on any occasion, is your first task. Impossible as this may sound, it can be done, and a simple technique will effect it for you.

Probably you (like almost everyone), with or without a preceding "hello", greet others and open conversation with them by using such worn stock phrases as: "How are you?"; "How's things?"; "How's business?"; "Nice day, isn't it?"; etc. In other words, there is no indication of whatever individuality you have as you greet people or open conversation with them,—yet as a self power you must have individuality at all times and make it be seen and heard in all you say and do.

In like manner, when it is the other who does the greeting you again use stock phrases in order to respond to him, and thus once more fail to indicate whatever individuality you have.

It is this routine use of stock phrases in our greetings and responses that caused some wit to remark that "automation is the talk in front of conversation." Most definitely, the talk we engage in "in front of conversation" is talk devoid of individuality. An automaton could well perform it for us. Have you ever tired of those phrases though and tried to supplant them?

3. Your supplanter must have an interest-arousing characteristic to give it life

Various means of supplanting the stock phrases used in greetings and responses are available to you (such as using a statement instead of a question; saying, "You look well!" instead of "How are you?") but most of them aren't a sufficient departure from the stock phrases and have the bad feature of themselves quickly becoming stock phrases also. For this reason, of all the individuality ideas proposed and tried, the best so far found is that which eliminates the customary opening interchange entirely.

The supplanter so used is nothing more than a short remark worded to indicate and arouse interest in a topic before naming it. Because it does this, and because it hints the topic bears on the person addressed, it's referred to as the "topic teaser" technique.

The "topic teaser" itself offers many advantages. First, it easily serves both as an opener and as a response. Further, when used as a response, it is one that can ignore another's meaningless opener without making the ignoring of it seem obviously deliberate. In addition, it heads off and dispenses with all tiresome preliminaries ("How's the wife?" "And the children?" Etc.) by arousing the other's interest or curiosity before he can start on them. Furthermore, and unlike other supplanters, it can be used on an individual, a group, or a large audience.

Because the "topic teaser" technique is not a "phrase formula," and because its "teaser" constantly changes and is new from day to day, it never deteriorates into a stock phrase or any equivalent of one. It is always new, different and individual. And its interest-arousing characteristic gives it life. Thus, for you, it projects individualism.

4. The "topic teaser" technique

The "topic teaser" technique can best be illustrated by showing you how some of the existing self powers use it. One of these, a business executive, makes it a matter of routine to decide on a new "teaser" as he is shaving each morning. When I last saw him his teaser for the day was, "Seeing you has reminded me of something." And it caught the interest or curiosity of everyone he said it to.

Where persons only exchanged a "good morning" with him as he passed them, he of course had no need of it, but, to everyone (even family and secretary) who went beyond a "good morning" and confronted him with a greeting ("How are you?" etc.), he instantly said, "Seeing you has reminded me of something." Every time he did it the other person or persons would immediately come out with a "What is it?," sound a curious "Oh?," or else interestedly wait silently "all ears" to hear what the something might be. He naturally had no prepared "something" but in every instance, as he uttered the teaser, he quickly conceived or invented a "something." Some were purposeful, some were newsy, and some were amusing. To his secretary he said, "Somehow your ingenuity will have to clear me a free hour in the middle of my afternoon appointment schedule." To a department executive he said, "If you could come up with a 'Search For Genius' contest for the employees it might be a good way to perk up their interest." To me he said, "Since you're my ghost now, when I'm dead will you still be my ghost or can I do my own haunting?"

Another self power gets a lot of enjoyment from his "teasers" and claims he milks a bonus benefit from his "teaser" devising. Instead of "counting sheep" or letting other problems engage his mind when he goes to bed at night, he devises "teasers"! He claims that that routine is a perfect sedative and that it enables him to devise his next day's teaser and fall into a sound sleep in minutes.

On a recent day his teaser was, "You're a problem." He had no preconceived problem or problems in mind as he said it, but, no matter who the person or group was that he said it to, he conceived a "problem" as he uttered the "teaser." When he said it to several friends who accosted him as he went to lunch he followed through with, "I was going to flip a coin to see which one of you should buy my lunch but I can't find a three-sided coin." When he used it as his opening words and greeting to a delegation of women he addressed during the afternoon ("Ladies, you're a problem!") it pulled them to attention instantly,—and he then won them completely by following through with, "You're too attractive; my eyes are going to be on you instead of my notes. How about letting me tear up my notes so I can enjoy you without distraction while I talk to you?" After the radiance and applause that pulled he could have recited nursery rhymes and held them!

5. The trick of the "topic teaser" technique

The trick that makes the "topic teaser" a success for you has three parts: (1) Constant change of the "teaser," a new one each day; (2) making the "teaser" be a statement (a *brief* one) that indicates that a topic of interest to and pertaining to your hearer may follow; (3) putting extra life in the "teaser" by making it sound spontaneous (letting it ring out as if prompted by a sudden thought or reaction that the other person or persons somehow brought on).

Constant change of the "teaser" is essential so don't neglect it. Unless you use a new one each day, your "teasers" can't be effective. (However, you can repeat most of them many times if you space the repeats at least a half dozen or more weeks apart, so that the "teasers" always have a newness.)

In instances where you have just used your "teaser" on someone and, while still talking to him, one or more others join you, you do not repeat your same "teaser." Instead, you hark back to "teasers" you have used on other days, and thus use a different "teaser" for each occasion of response.

The devising of a new "teaser" each day may sound like work, and for the first several weeks it easily may be, but you will soon find that each "teaser" suggests new possibilities and also that the rewards from them make their cost negligible. Try one tomorrow and see what happens. And don't put it off because you have trouble devising your first one. If you can't think of a good one in a hurry, borrow one of those mentioned in the examples!

6. The body of your talk and conversation needs to have a living individuality also

The second of the ways in which you can make a fluid inventory of phrases and material project individualism for you was pointed out as that of eliminating stock phrases and worn material from the body or text of your actual talking, speaking and conversing.

Whether you are very conscious of it or not, you, like everyone, have many stock phrases that occur again and again in your talk, your conversation, your letters and your speeches.

Some of these may be strictly your own, but in the main they aren't. Most of them are phrases that many others use again and again also. These latter are the detracting ones, and it is on them you need to focus your attention.

Phrases that are strictly your own, that are characteristics of expression peculiar to you, are as much a part of you as are your unconscious mannerisms. They in like manner contribute to your individuality, so don't tamper with or eliminate them. (Unless you are given to badly overworking them!) Let them alone and don't let yourself become too conscious of them.

At this time you are concerned with only one thing, the putting of the same living individuality into the body of your talk and conversation as you have now put into your greetings and responses, so that it too will project individualism for you.

7. Eliminate set phrases, particularly the commonly abused and ill-used ones

For your first move toward eliminating stock phrases from your talk, conversation, letters and speeches, try to note those set phrases you find yourself using daily. Usually these will be phrases such as, perhaps so; it's my guess that; by the way; in the interim; let it pass; okay; etc.

At the same time, particularly note (and mark for *complete* eradication) those phrases that have been so ill-used by people in general that their use now would identify you with the lower cultural levels (You said it! But definitely! Don't give me that! Hope to tell you! You bet! Baloney! Know what I mean? Knocked me for a loop. That sort of stuff. Yeah, man! Etc.).

Possibly it would be well to point out right here that slang, when it is of the nature of an idiom, or isn't abused, is well accepted and has its place and purpose. However, abused slang (bat the breeze; dish it out; flip your lid; lots of guts; etc.), just like abused words (corny, hot, cool, dope, etc.), should be used with caution and never in the sense or manner that the abusers of it employ. (Attention markedly has not been called here to uncouth, vulgar and obscene words, terms and expressions because it is assumed you had on your own lifted yourself above all such and abandoned them when you set yourself apart from people and began your building of self power.)

The phrases you note are the ones you need to eliminate. Whether they are merely set phrases, ill-used ones, abused ones, or what they are, search them out constantly. If you don't, as you eliminate some of them from your talk, others will creep in.

8. Set phrases are used more because of carelessness or laziness than because of any fitness

It should not be necessary for you to make written note of all the stock phrases you want to eliminate, but in some instances it may help. This is applicable most of all to your next move which calls for you to devise at least one alternate for each of those phrases.

A word of caution: When you devise an alternate, don't "pick another phrase" nor fasten upon your alternate as a full-time substitute for the phrase you are abandoning. If you do, the alternate will quickly become a stock phrase itself! Your purpose in devising the alternate is not to concoct a substitute but to remind yourself of at least one other way of saying the thought and conveying your meaning. Usually it will prove to be a better way, and in all instances it will allow individuality.

When you note a phrase and try to devise an alternate, there is a good chance you'll find the phrase to be eliminated was only a habit and that it often conveyed no meaning or at least not the intended one. By way of illustrating this: One executive used "in the interim" so much that his employees spoke of him as "Mr. Interim." When he set out to eliminate the phrase he found that, in most instances of his use of it, it had no application whatever. ("Make those corrections and in the interim get Jones for me." "Cancel my luncheon appointment and in the interim have some lunch brought in for me." "Take the rest of the day off and in the interim try to get rid of that cold.")

Though your purpose in devising the alternate is to remind yourself of other ways of saying the thought and conveying your meaning, the devising of the alternate also serves another purpose. Providing you truly devise an alternate and don't just grab at a substitute phrase, as you try to devise the alternate you will find that no one alternate can be used everywhere you heretofore used the phrase. Thus, devising of the alternate will call to your attention and point up that you used the set phrase more because of carelessness or laziness on your part than because of its fitness.

9. Devising the alternate serves as your corrective technique

What is the technique for using a fluid inventory of phrases in place of stock phrases? There is none and you need none; your elimination of the stock phrases automatically compels you to be conscious of what it is your intent to say and, by not allowing you use of an indefinite multi-purpose expression, it forces you to say it more individually and precisely!

10. New material makes you an interesting source and adds to projection of your individualism

The same procedure you have used on phrases will produce like results when applied to your conversational material. It will make your conversation take on life and be newly interesting.

In the same manner that you focused attention on phrases, focus attention on how shopworn much of your conversational material is. Most of it you will find is so used and overused by you that anyone who knows you well knows pretty much beforehand what material you will introduce into and use in various conversations. (Just as you know the same of them!) And this is true whether the conversations are social, business, or what they are.

During the next three days, take the trouble to note what

your conversational material is in every conversation in which you engage. You will find that with certain people (certain associates, customers, fellow commuters, neighbors, family, etc.) your conversational material is almost always the same. With one of them the weather supplies the material; with another the stock market; with another the happenings or people at the office; and so it goes, day after day, routinely "making talk" by unloading thoughts without considering whether the other is truly interested in them (and he does the same!). What makes all this even worse, you (and they) adhere day after day to a single pattern in discussion of the shopworn material!

If pointing these things out sounds like a condemnation of routine conversation, it isn't. Routine conversation serves a purpose. It lets people congenially pass the time while in the company of each other. But, for you, that isn't enough.

While you congenially pass the time in the company of others you need to still be a self power, a distinctively individual one, one that projects individualism. To do that, you can't be routine or commonplace in your conversation,—you must have individuality even while engaging in conversation.

11. The tidbit technique

There are many ways you can avail yourself of new conversational material. One of the best ways is to daily pick several unusual or hidden (not sensational or headlined) news stories and editorials from newspapers and magazines and to put those forth as tidbits that will interest whomever you talk to. Pick several of these tidbits each day. No matter what they pertain to, the chances are high that they will prove to be more interesting conversational material than that which you routinely have used or been drawn into.

As an example of what these tidbits can be, here are the six that one self power used on a recent day: (1) The pay of teachers, when converted to a per hour rate, exceeds that of the chemists and physicists employed on top research projects. (2) An international currency could be the key to world peace. (3) Insurance dollars depreciate more than any other "investment" dollar. (4) Changing trends are putting "white elephants" in the pink. (5) We need a third party to cure the ills of our two party system. (6) In winter, the all-electric home can be a death-trap.

Few people will ever need to arm themselves with six tidbits per day. However, whether it is two, three or six you need, arm yourself with them and use one or more of them in each instance where your conversation or talk would otherwise use shopworn material or follow a routine pattern.

That in itself will help you, but as you day by day come forth with constantly new material, everyone, even your family, will see you differently than they ever have in the past. All of them will develop a new appreciation of you and regard you as a distinctively individual, interesting and non-routine conversationalist. They will see you and look to you as an unending source of new conversational material for themselves! And through all this, your tidbits will be projecting individualism for you.

12. Points worth special attention

1. Putting life into your individuality gives you a more distinctively individual quality.

2. Because conventional greetings and responses are devoid of individuality you must eliminate them.

3. Use the "topic teaser" technique as your opener; arouse interest with it and head off meaningless preliminaries.

4. Change your "teaser" at least once each day.

5. Make it ring out as if prompted by a sudden thought or reaction that the other person or persons somehow brought on.

6. Overworked phrases are used more because of carelessness or laziness than because of any fitness.

7. Because ill-used, abused and set phrases detract from your individuality and self power image, you must eliminate them.

8. The devising of alternates for such phrases is your best corrective technique.

9. Because shopworn conversational material makes you commonplace, you must displace it; never offer it and avoid being drawn into it.

10. Use the tidbit technique to make every conversation have newness and interest.

13

HOW TO MAKE YOUR THINKING WIN

If you don't "hog" the thinking, you can make your thinking win when you need to.

Three courses are open to you for making your thinking win.

Neither the "hard sell" nor "soft sell" have merit by self power standards.

When you push, suggest or argue your thinking you reduce your self power.

Using the "think puller" technique you can make your thinking win without losing anything.

The "this not that" trick is the key to making your thinking win.

Through building and expanding your individuality you are constantly increasing your self power. And you have been lifted by it. Showing people that you speak your own mind, and that neither what you say nor how you say it is commonplace, has put you at a new elevation in everyone's regard. People are seeing you as a distinctive thinker and as a source of thoughts. They are interested. But they have thoughts too. Whether they express them or not, and whether they originate them or not, they have them.

131

1. Don't "hog" the thinking; make your thinking win only when you need to

You are projecting an individualism that all people like. The more of it you project, the more self power you emanate. And the more self power you emanate, the more do people listen to you. But also, the more attentively and critically do many of them listen to you.

At times, their thoughts won't coincide with yours, and much of the time that will be of little or no importance. However, there will be times when you will need to have people think as you do. What you must do now is make sure that when those times come, your thinking will win.

Right here you come to another fork in your road. Earlier, when you were deciding your aims and what path could reach them for you, you had to choose between the fellowship path and the self power path. Now you have come to a place where three roads are open to you. And again you must decide what your aims are and which road can reach them for you. In different manners, and to different kinds of success, you can make your thinking win when need be by pushing with it, pulling with it, or coasting and sliding with it.

The words "when need be" should not be overlooked. If you try to make your thinking win when unnecessary, the people you need most will turn away from you, seeing you as more a despot than a self power. On the other hand (and so long as you do not "hog" the thinking), because you are a self power, most people are going to have a sympathetic and respectful regard for your thinking. As a result, except in unusual instances, they'll "go along" with you even when they don't think exactly as you do. And most times that is all you need. However, when their thinking is undecided, or is contrary to yours, on something that is important to your aims, you have an instance where you need to make your thinking win.

2. Self power standards, not "sales standards," must determine whether you hard sell, indirect sell or soft sell your thinking

When you need to make your thinking win, three courses are open to you: (1) You can push people's thinking to make it go where you want it to go; or (2) you can pull people's thinking to draw it to where you want it to be; or (3) you can seemingly neglect their thinking, act content that they listen to yours and then take your chances on yours (or your arguments for it) being recognized and accepted as better than their own or someone else's.

In one way or another, and to varying degrees, you already are daily using some or all of those roads. You use one or another of them each time you put forth a thought, argument, proposal, theory or opinion. The roads have different names in different fields, but they are most commonly known by the names salesmen, politicians, ecclesiastics, lecturers and advertising men use for them,—hard sell, indirect sell, and soft sell. No matter what you heretofore have called them, from here on when you apply them to yourself think of them only as the push road, pull road and flat road, and weigh their merits by self power standards, not by customary "sales power" standards.

3. Human factors cause the push road to bring you a percentage of sure success

People in general use the push road most of all. They do it firstly because they like to tell people what and how to think, secondly because they find it easier to tell people than to convince people, and thirdly because they know a certain percentage of people (a) always can be pushed, (b) never or rarely think for themselves, or (c) even wait to be pushed and are always ready to let the strongest pusher push them.

You are well acquainted with how advertising uses the push

road: "Buy twozies today; two-to-one better for you." And how politicians, etc., use it: "You don't want a dole, you want compensation and security!" But it is used just as much in general talk and conversation: "You don't want to get there early and have to wait for the others."

No matter who uses the push road or how, it always is effective on some people. However, just how effective it is, and on how many it is effective, is determined more by the power of the push (or pusher) than by the merit or value of the thought that is pushed.

Because this last is true, and also for the reasons that people in general use the push road, you, like all people who acquire power (whether self power, agency power, or any other), are going to be tempted to use the push road each time you find people are closely attentive to what you say. Let's acknowledge right now that if you do use it, you will be successful with it (percentagewise, your thinking will win), and you will push the thinking of many people who only a few yesterdays ago weren't even heedful that you could be an individual!

But those things aren't your only consideration. If they were you could make your decision now and disregard that alternate roads are available to you.

4. The more push power you use, the more you reduce your self power

Immediately you choose the push road, those who are attentive to you become less passive and definitely react, either favorably or unfavorably. Your push, by the reactions it stirs, separates them into three distinct groups. One of these is the group that accepts your pushing (and, because you are a self power, this group is a goodly sized one). Another of the groups is composed of the persons who "just don't like to be pushed" (whether the pushing is physical or mental, they plant their feet firmly and just won't budge, even though the pusher is trying to push them in the direction they had intended to go). The third group, but probably second largest, is composed of those persons whom pushing antagonizes (they are converted to adversaries by your push, though they were among your favorers before you pushed them).

Since you are a self power, and you are aiming for maximum effectiveness of your self power, you cannot afford to deliberately provoke unfavorable reactions. The push road does that, and for this reason you can't afford to use it (nor any road that will create those second and third groups and remove them from your power, influence and control). As a consequence, regardless of how highly you appraise the push road, and despite what merit you think the hard sell may have by customary "sales power" standards, you must avoid all personal use of it.

If you are a dyed-in-the-wool "hard sell" enthusiast it may be hard for you to abandon it. However, before stubbornly saying you won't, take a look at the two alternate roads that are available to you and then decide which will best achieve your aims and make you more effective as a self power.

5. The flat road has neither the advantages nor disadvantages of the push road

Day to day, and for all purposes (talking, conversing, selling, advertising, etc), the flat road is used almost as much as is the push road. And like the push road, it has both advantages and disadvantages

When you use the flat road, you don't tell people what and how to think As a result, when you use it you eliminate the biggest advantage of the push road, but you at the same time eliminate its biggest disadvantage also. In other words, when you use the flat road you don't automatically catch that die-cut group of persons who are ready, willing and wanting to be pushed, and neither do you create that antagonistic group who rebel against and combat a push.

That weighs well, but now let's look at the flat road's other advantages and disadvantages. Like the push road, it has some of each and a decision that didn't weigh all of them wouldn't be worth much.

6. Human factors assure the flat road of a percentage of success also

On the flat road, instead of telling people how to think, you supposedly merely assert thinking and put forth arguments in favor of it, but actually you suggest that that thinking should be the thinking of the reader or hearers. You are accustomed to the many ways in which advertising does this: Manny Mead says, "I use twozies regularly, because like millions of others I think they are two-to-one better." And you know how politicians use it: "I look on a dole as charity; I think instead of charity you should be given compensation and security!" In conversation it works the same: "I think if I were in your place I wouldn't want to get there early; it would mean having to wait for the others."

Like with the push, no matter who uses the flat road or how, it always is effective on some people. Unlike the push, though, with it effectiveness is more dependent on the hearers' regard of the one to whom the thought is credited (or on the strength of the arguments for the thought) than it is on the force with which the thought is put forth.

Once again, and both because these things are true and because you are a self power, let's acknowledge that if you use the flat road you will be successful with it (percentagewise, your thinking will win). And here too, many persons who a few yesterdays ago weren't heedful you could be an individual, will be won to your thinking.

But once more those things aren't your only consideration and you don't dare make your decision on them alone.

7. Any argument or suggestion that can be resisted reduces your self power

The instant you choose the flat road, those who are at all attentive to you are separated by your suggestiveness into three distinguishable groups. One group is somewhat comparable to the first of your push groups and is made up of "followers" (mostly persons who would rather follow someone else's thinking than to do or trust their own). A second group, very comparable to your second push group, is made up of "stand-patters" (persons who like to feel they have "sales resistance" and therefor hold back from going along with your thinking even though they have no substitute or reason to offer; some among them are persons who set their minds against "argument" but others of them just don't think). The third group, and usually the smallest, consists mainly of persons who think contrarily (but it also includes those few that "couldn't see" your arguments).

As you can see, though the flat road doesn't have the advantages and disadvantages of the push road, it displaces them with advantages and disadvantages of its own. It's "advantage" group may be greater or less great, but its second and third groups, though more resistive than opposive in character, again are groups that have ceased to react favorably.

As said earlier, since you are a self power and are aiming for maximum effectiveness of your self power, you can't afford to use any road that will create those second and third groups and remove them from your power, influence and control. Thus, as before, regardless of how highly you appraise the flat road, and despite what merit you think the soft sell may have by customary "sales power" standards, you must avoid all personal use of it. As a self power you can't afford to use any hard sell or soft sell (in your speaking, conversing, letter writing, memos, etc.) when you need to make your thinking win, so look now toward the one alternate road that remains available to you.

8. Use of the pull road gives you an opportunity to win without losing anything

The pull road is a very little used road and most people have no acquaintance with it whatever. Though salesmen, advertisers, and many others refer to it as an "indirect sell," it in many respects is the most direct, and especially in the sense that it deals more personally with your hearers than do the other two methods while making your thinking win.

When you use the pull road, instead of telling people how to think, or suggesting a thinking and arguing for it, you draw on the person's own thinking (even though actually you subtly or indirectly suggest it) and then inconspicuously guide its direction.

The pull road is comparatively seldom used in advertising but you are sure to have seen it nevertheless: "When you wished for something twice as good, you supplied the idea for twozies; if you really think they're two-to-one better we'll know it by how you buy them." And politicians of course use it even more seldomly than do advertisers: "Is it your thought that a dole is your due, or is it compensation and security that you want?" When the pull is used in conversation, the pull is quite often much less subtle: "In saying you want to get there early, I suppose you mean early enough not to be late but not so early you'd have to wait for the others."

Though the pull only indirectly attributes a line of thinking, the mere fact that it voices a line of thinking causes it to pull those same persons who in the main make up group one of the push road and group one of the flat road (the persons who never or rarely think for themselves and want thinking to be set forth for them). Thus, without pushing, and without suggesting or arguing, the pull road accomplishes the best that those can accomplish.

In addition, and because the pull doesn't dictate, suggest or argue any thinking, it can't provoke resistance or opposition to you. Therefor, it has none of the unfavorable features that both the push and flat roads have. Seen in this way, the pull road has the advantages of the push road and flat road without having any of their disadvantages and is the one road that gives you a chance to win without losing anything.

9. The "think puller" technique

The pull road is free of ordinary disadvantages and the only things you might look on as disadvantages of it are the following: (a) It isn't as easy a road as the other two and (b) it's a less natural one (therefor you can't launch it as spontaneously or "off the cuff"). However, the "think puller" technique solves these problems for you.

Reduced to the fewest words, the "think puller" technique is this: (1) Put forth thinking in such a manner that *it must be accepted or rejected* (never so that it can be resisted, combatted or argued); (2) indicate the thinking has merit; (3) though the thinking is the thinking you want to win (the thinking you want your hearers to achieve), *put it forth entirely as being your hearers' thinking,* never as your own.

In every instance, as you put the thinking forth you must indicate you assume it is your hearers thinking,—and must indirectly imply that you think as they do.

No matter what the thinking is, and no matter whether your hearers accept or reject it, when you put the thinking forth in this manner it perks the pride of people that *you* think as *they* do,—whereas, with the thinking put forth otherwise, numbers of them might forever be reluctant to admit they think as *you* do.

The "think puller" technique is simple and easy but, preliminary to any exercise of it, it requires that you (1) never engage in argument *with anyone you want to pull to your thinking,* (2) never argue thinking you want to win, and (3) never dispute the thinking put forth by one whom you want to pull to your thinking.

10. Use the "think puller" both to invent thinking and to turn thinking about

The "think puller" technique, as the examples already given have illustrated, contrives another's words for him so that they say what *you* want him to say.

You won't always have an opportunity to contrive another's thinking before he has stated it so you must be ready at all times to approach your pull from either of two directions and to use the technique in the way it fits. For example: (a) When the other (your hearer or hearers) has not put forth a thought, you must take what you want him to think and (instead of pushing or telling him to think it) put the thought into words that make it *his* thought with you merely voicing it for him. (b) When the other *has* put forth a thought and his thinking is not what you want it to be, you must (instead of arguing or disputing it) *turn his words around* for him so they are able to say for him what you want him to say.

Where the situation is that given in (a) you have no problem. You can use either a statement or a question to make the pull. By way of illustration: "Since you govern your mind instead of letting some politician dictate it, I assume it is your thinking that taxes should be dealt with on a profit and loss basis instead of on a spend and tax basis." And, "Is it your opinion that government can't be run on a business basis, or is it your thinking that government should be compelled to abide by the same rules it establishes for corporations instead of being allowed to flout every sound and common sense principle?"

Where the situation is that given in (b), most times the contriving of the pull is as simple as the already given example demonstrates: "In saying you want to get there early, I suppose you mean early enough not to be late but not so early you'd have to wait for the others." Occasionally, however, your contriving of the pull is made a little more difficult by a statement that doesn't easily turn.

As an illustration of the "not easily turned" statement and of the handling of it: Another might say something such as, "I think our new model should be priced lower." You don't need to ask him why; you know why he thinks so. And arguing won't change his thinking. Neither will disputing it or challenging it. But you still want him to think and say that the new model should be priced higher, not lower. You could say, "Good. If I read your thinking properly, it isn't your thought that we should ignore our increased material and production costs as we price our new model, but that, in adjusting to the increased costs, if we could see to it that our new model is priced lower than competitive ones, increased sales might offset the lost profit percentage. Is that right?"

11. Your skill with the "this not that" trick makes your thinking win

The trick of the "think puller" technique should already be obvious to you. It lies in putting forth two opposing thoughts for the other (this one meritorious, that one not) and crediting him always with thinking "this, not that."

The trick isn't difficult. In almost every instance all you need do is take two opposing thoughts that you would use if you were arguing your thinking, and then, instead of arguing your thinking with them, put them forth as the "this not that" of the other's thinking!

How well and how often you are able to make your thinking win depends first of all on how consistently you use the "think puller" technique (instead of the customary push road and flat road) to bring others to your thinking. It depends second on your success with the technique, and that in turn always depends on one thing,—your skill with the "this not that" trick.

12. Points worth special attention

1. So long as you do not "hog" the thinking, most people will have a sympathetic and respectful regard for your thinking and "go along" with you.

2. If you try to make your thinking win when unnecessary, people will see you more a despot than a self power.

3. Self power standards only (not "sales power" standards) must determine the method you use.

4. You cannot afford to use any method that may provoke people to oppose or resist your thinking.

5. When you tell people how to think, suggest what they should think, or argue they should think something, you provoke a percentage of them to resist or oppose you.

6. When you provoke people to resist or oppose you, you remove them from your power, influence and control.

7. The pull road is the only one that gives you an opportunity to win without losing anything.

8. Use the "think puller" technique so that you can contrive another's thinking and make it his own.

9. The "think puller" perks the pride of people by letting them see you as thinking as they do (though they would be reluctant to admit they think as you do).

10. Never engage in argument with any you want to pull to your thinking; never argue the thinking you want to win; and never dispute the thinking put forth by any you want to pull to your thinking.

11. When another has put forth thinking that is other than you want it to be, turn his words around for him so they are able to say for him what you want him to say.

12. Always put forth two opposing thoughts for the other, as this one meritorious and that one not, so that you are crediting him with thinking "this, not that."

13. Your skill with the "this not that" trick determines what success you will have with making your thinking win.

14

HOW TO PULL MAXIMUM COOPERATIVENESS

What motivates cooperation determines its value and dependability.

Feigned cooperation, and cooperation with ulterior motives,
must be recognized and rejected.

Compulsory, enticed and obliged cooperation are drawn
forth by your agency or buying power, not by you.

Common interest cooperation is the most valuable and
dependable.

Making partisans of people draws them into common
interest cooperation.

The "let's" technique and the "you we" technique help you
make partisans of people.

When you break yourself of thoughtlessness you pull a
maximum of common interest cooperativeness from every
quarter.

Every step you have taken has made you more aware that
no one ever has self power as "a gift" or by accident. At the same
time, each step has also made you increasingly aware of the
tremendous difference there is between self power and mere
agency power. Because of these things, you should be stronger
than ever in your aims and should by now be seeing them as
things soon to be realized.

143

1. You need every little crumb of cooperation that is within your reach

Your self power has pulled a lot of people toward you and and it is pulling more each day. You need them, all of them, and you need things from them. They are giving you friendly and favorable notice and they are being attentive to you. They are pleasant to you and in various ways they are showing themselves as ready and willing to please you. You are enjoying more cooperativeness from people than you have ever known before. All you need do now is open a little wider to people and they will bend still further and give you a maximum of cooperativeness.

Don't jump to the conclusion here that everyone who does your bidding is being cooperative. There is a big difference between having people compliantly do your bidding and having them cooperatively look to your wishes. And likewise, don't conclude that others are being cooperative just because they. "go along" with you, on your whims, ideas or anything else. There is a big difference between those who "go along" merely by not opposing you and those who "go along" by cooperatively joining in with you.

All the things you so far have knit together for your self power are bringing you more than ordinary cooperativeness. Nevertheless, there is still more of it you can go after and get. You want and need every little crumb of it that is within your reach. Your job now is to get those crumbs.

2. There are four ways you can go after cooperation

As you go after those extra crumbs of cooperativeness there are some more cold facts you must widen your eyes to and face. Cooperation can be honest or dishonest, real or feigned, open in its motives or ulterior in its motives. Whether you like to face the fact or not, you must. You can never be an effective self power unless you have the courage to appraise the character of cooperation and to reject all that is dishonest, feigned, or ulterior in its motives.

And there is still one further fact you must face. Honest, real and open cooperation is not all of one type either. By those things that motivate it, it divides itself into four different types and as a result there are four ways you can go after it and get it. One is by compelling it, another is by enticing it, another is by obliging it, and a fourth is by opening a path for it and drawing people into willingly giving it.

3. The value and dependability of any cooperation depends on what motivates it

At this point is would be well to draw a clear line between the four types of cooperation so as to dispose of compulsory, enticed and obliged cooperation once and for all and eliminate them from what is meant when we hereafter refer to willful cooperativeness.

Any time cooperation is forced, and no matter how indirectly it is forced, it must be looked upon as compulsory cooperation. For example: If another supposedly "voluntarily" cooperates, but does so only because you could force him to cooperate if he didn't do so "voluntarily," the cooperation you get from him still must be looked to as compulsory cooperation. For this reason, don't be too quick to pat yourself on the back when someone "voluntarily" cooperates with you. If he has done it because you are in control or are affluent or are the boss, he hasn't been motivated by a will to be cooperative; his cooperation has been drawn forth by your agency power, not by you.

Similarly, any time cooperation is "bought," and no matter how indirectly, it must be looked upon as enticed cooperation. This applies wherever another supposedly "voluntarily" cooperates, but does so only because he expects to reap some reward for it. For example, even when you have promised nothing, you must look to the following as enticed cooperation: Cooperation given to you in expectation you will return the favor; cooperation given to you in expectation of your patronage, of a tip, or the like; campaign cooperation in hope of an appointment or other benefit; etc. Thus again, don't be too quick to pat yourself on the back when someone "voluntarily" cooperates with you. If he has done it in hopes of a reward, he hasn't been motivated by a will to be cooperative; knowingly or unknowingly you have indirectly bought his cooperation and it has been drawn forth by your "buying" power, not by you.

Obliged cooperation is of course "bought" cooperation but of a slightly different type. For example: When you so flatter a person that he or she feels obliged to cooperate with you, or when a person cooperates with you because he or she feels obliged to do so in return for or in consequence of something else, the cooperation must always be looked upon solely as "bought" cooperation. It too is cooperation drawn forth by your "buying" power, not by you.

Many a would-be self power has made his first big mistake in his failure to differentiate between the cooperation that is compulsory, enticed or obliged and that which is entirely willful. If you are going to be an effective self power you can't afford to close your mind to the difference. No matter how much a blow it is to your ego to do so, always see compulsory, enticed and obliged "voluntary" cooperation as being exactly what they are instead of crediting yourself with them. Recognize that *the value and dependability of any cooperation depends on what motivates it.*

4. Be practical and realistic in your use and valuing of cooperation

What has just been said doesn't mean that you should cease to be practical. To the contrary, it means you must be more of a realist. It doesn't mean you should disdain all not genuinely voluntary cooperation; it only means that you must clearly recognize it as what it is and judge its value and dependability accordingly.

This same applies also to all so-called "out-of-the-goodness-of-their-hearts" cooperation. Some of this is of the "friendly" or "neighborly" type, given solely or mostly because of a kindliness of feeling toward you and very little because of actual common interest in the thing being done. Other of it is of the "good Samaritan" type, given particularly in instances of emergency, disaster, etc., because of sympathy with your plight or task.

No matter what type the cooperation is that others are motivated to give you "out of the goodness of their hearts," it certainly is fully voluntary cooperation and as such is usually (but not always!) welcome. However, it too must in every instance be recognized as being exactly what it is. The very fact that it is "out-of-the-goodness-of-their-hearts" cooperation causes it to be of whimsical character and makes it a cooperation that you cannot always count upon. Therefor, here again be a realist; accept it and appreciate it when you get it and can use it, but don't falsely value it or depend on it.

5. Build common interest cooperation in every way you can

The cooperation you need, and the one that is of most value to you and is most dependable, is that which is motivated solely by a will to be partisanly cooperative. Very little of cooperation is ever of this type, but you must go after it nevertheless and generate and build it wherever you can. So that it cannot be confused with other types, from here on it will be referred to as common interest cooperation.

Common interest cooperation is more free, more sincere, more ready, and of a more lasting quality than cooperation that results from people liking you, feeling sorry for you, fearing you, kowtowing to you, feeling obliged to you or seeking reward from you. And it is made so by the simple fact that common interest, either inherent or generated, is what motivates it.

Rare as common interest cooperation is, it is easy to generate and build if you set about it in the right way. All you need do is to treat people as partisans and open up the opportunity for them to be partisans.

6. Never give orders unnecessarily and avoid wording them as commands wherever possible

In general, people welcome every opportunity of partisanship you open to them. However, even those who don't can usually be pulled to it. The things it takes are little things, but they are ones that work against you as big things when they are missing.

When you go after people's cooperation, your first job is to make sure nothing in your own manner or habits will hinder your getting it; you can't pull people toward partisanship while anything in the words or tone you use on them puts a foot on their necks or downgrades them. To see how much this means, look at the things that in the past have caused you to be stand-offish with your own cooperation and you will see the things that can hinder your getting cooperation now.

You are aware of your own reactions to people who order, command, "teach," dictate, etc. (and you have already been given most of the techniques for dealing with them), but you must make yourself equally aware that other persons react as adversely to those things as you do. Be conscious at all times that when any of those things are in your words or tone, no amount of politeness or good intent you try to give them can change their effect. In short, remind yourself constantly that *a foot on some-one's neck, no matter how lightly or politely it's put there, is still a foot on his neck and will always disincline him from cooperating with you.*

To get cooperation then, the first rule is: Never give orders unnecessarily. And the second rule is: When you must give an order, wherever possible avoid wording it as a command; word it to state joint interest in what is imperative or word it as either a request or decision puller.

7. The "let's" technique

No matter what your executive or supervisory status is, there are probably at least a few times each day when you must tell someone to do something. Except in cases of extreme emergency (occasioned by mishap, etc.), the telling usually doesn't need to be done commandingly. As a consequence, the instance is rare where it is not possible for you to word your order as something less than one yet equally effective.

Most of your orders, whether barked as commands or spoken pleasantly, are brief sentences (close the door; put this in the mail today; raise the temperature on the drying bins; change that to red; hold off on that shipment; etc.).

When any of your brief sentences doesn't need a "you" or "your" in it, the tacking of "let's" on the front of it is all that is needed to convert it to a statement of joint interest (let's close the door; let's put this in the mail today; etc.). Trivial as this conversion might seem, it works magic for you. Develop the "let's" habit and you will generate a lot more common interest cooperation.

In instances where your order is a multiple one, really two or three orders combined as one (finish that paint job in a hurry and then get the floor cleaned up right away), you need to tack the "let's" on each of its parts (let's finish that paint job in a hurry and then let's get the floor cleaned up right away).

8. Substitute "would you" wherever joint interest can't easily be shown

With but two exceptions, you should use the "let's" technique (or a self-devised equivalent of it) wherever you can. One exception (dealt with in the section that follows) is where your order would be voicing the obvious. The other is where your brief sentence needs to include a "you" or "your" in it (take your feet off the desk; see if you can find their file). With sentences such as these it is usually better to forego the "let's" and to convert the order to a request by using a "would you" as an opener for it (would you take your feet off the desk; would you see if you can find their file).

Occasionally, particularly in sentences that would contain a "for me" (get Jones on the phone for me; put this away for me), you have a choice. You can either tack on "let's" and drop the "for me" (let's get Jones on the phone; let's put this away), or you can simply make use of the "would you" (would you get Jones on the phone for me; would you put this away for me).

In general, then, wherever joint interest can't easily be shown, forego the "let's" and use "would you" as a substitute.

9. The "you we" technique

Many times the order you give is one that voices the obvious (shut it down and repair it; give them a rest; make the lids fit better). Where this is the case, never tack "let's" on it.

When the obvious is being dealt with, often your hearer looks upon a remark headed by "let's" as one indirectly criticising him for not having already done the thing mentioned (let's shut it down and repair it; let's give them a rest; let's make the lids fit better). For this reason, in every instance where your order would be voicing the obvious, something other than the "let's" technique needs to be used.

The "you we" technique is your best converter in all cases of this kind. By tacking a "don't you think we should" on the front of your order it converts the order from a command to a decision puller. And, since you are dealing with the obvious, you have a lot to gain and nothing to lose by calling on your hearer to make a decision (don't you think we should shut it down and repair it; don't you think we should give them a rest; don't you think we should make the lids fit better).

10. Use equivalents for variety, but choose and fit them carefully

The "let's" and "you we" techniques (and the "would you" alternate) are the only ones set forth here because they are the easiest to use and the most dependable. However, many equivalents of them exist and are frequently used (suppose we; shall we; wonder if we; couldn't we; perhaps we; etc.). These equivalents are less all-purpose but they can provide variety.

In using these or any self-devised equivalents, make sure you use them only where they will fit. For example: "Suppose we close the door" often could be as effective as "let's close the door," but "suppose we put this in the mail today" never is as effective as "let's put this in the mail today."

A word of caution: Never try to use the word "please" as an equivalent. "Please" has its place when properly used with specific requests but it boomerangs when you try to use it to soften a command or to turn an order into a request. When used in front of or behind an order, it commonly has the effect of making the order more imperiously commanding (please close the door; close the door please; please put this in the mail today; put this in the mail today please). To guard against this, never use "please" in an attempt to soften or convert an order!

11. Break yourself of thoughtlessness and you'll pull common interest cooperativeness

As said earlier, the "let's" and "you we" and all their equivalents are seemingly little things, but they are ones that work against you as big things when they are missing.

Orders seldom need to be put forth as commands or dictates. When you state something as an order (no matter how softly or politely), you more often do so thoughtlessly or out of carelessness than out of necessity. Use the "let's" and "you we" techniques to break yourself of that and you will make partisans of people and immediately begin pulling a maximum of common interest cooperativeness from every quarter.

12. Points worth special attention

1. You need every little crumb of cooperation that is within your reach.

2. All those who do your bidding or "go along" with you are not necessarily cooperating with you.

3. Be quick to recognize and reject all cooperation that is dishonest, feigned, or ulterior in its motives.

4. See compulsory, enticed and obliged cooperation as being exactly what they are, even when they are supposedly "voluntary."

5. Always be mindful of the fact that the value and dependability of any cooperation is determined by what motivates it.

6. Never depend on "out-of-the-goodness-of-their-hearts" cooperation but welcome it when you can use it.

7. Common interest cooperation is more valuable and dependable than any other; build it in every way you can.

8. Treat people as partisans and most of them will seize the opportunity to be partisans.

9. Never give orders unnecessarily; word necessary orders to state a joint interest wherever possible.

10. Use the "let's" technique (or a fitting equivalent) everywhere possible.

11. Never give an order that voices the obvious; instead use the "you we" technique to convert the order to a decision puller.

12. Never use "please" in an attempt to soften or convert an order; it most often boomerangs.

13. The "let's" and "you we" are only important little things when you use them but they are big ones that work against you when you don't.

15

HOW TO BUILD THE VIGOR OF YOUR SELF POWER

Whenever self power recognizes or accepts limits it begins to wane.

Little things that build the vigor of your self power push it beyond every limit it might tend to have.

Increased exposure of your self power is the key to the building of its vigor.

The keys to the exposure techniques are "circulate," "travel" and "vary."

The more ingenuity you put into increasing your self power's exposure, the more you build its vigor.

Little thing after little thing has been put together by you and forged into self power. At one point in the forging you had to look ahead and see yourself as already being the self power you were forging. Now you are that self power. But you haven't reached the top of your climb; you are on the landing that many mistake for the top, but for you it's just the turn in the stairs. It has brought you to those last steps that rise above the "almost" and the little self powers and take you to the top.

153

1. Keep building the vigor of your self power so it can't stagnate or deteriorate

The effectiveness of your self power is increasing every day. Each day your skill with all the little things that combine to make it is increasing and, as a consequence, your power, influence and control over all those you work with, associate with and come in contact with is increasing each day too. You feel and know it is greater today than it was yesterday,—and you know it will be greater tomorrow than it is today. But any day now it will reach its maximum with those people. What then?

The first answer is: You can never let that maximum be a maximum. *The maximum of anything is an end point and you can't let your self power have an end point.* If you do, like anything else, when it reaches that end point it will either stagnate there or deteriorate.

The second answer is: You can't achieve your aims with self power that is stagnated or deteriorating. *You must build your self power's vigor and keep building it so that it pushes on and on beyond all maximums and every barrier that determines them.* You can do it, and the self power you already have built is the only equipment you need.

2. To prevent the waning of your effectiveness you must push beyond your regular contacts

The vigor of your self power comes from two things: It comes first from the quantity of self power you emanate, and it comes next from the quantity of people who see, feel and are affected by your self power.

Your skill with the self power techniques is increasing every day and, by so doing, is increasing the amount of self power you emanate. On the other hand, for the most part you are seeing and associating with the same people day in and day out and it therefor is only those same ones (a fixed quantity) that are seeing, feeling and being affected by your self power.

That fixed quantity is your problem,—you can't let it stay a fixed quantity. Once your self power has reached its maximum with those people it will begin to lose some of its effectiveness, —unless those people see its scope as not limited to them and as extending farther and farther beyond them. Thus, whatever that fixed quantity is, whether it numbers in the dozens or in the thousands, *you must push beyond it.*

3. Exposure to more and more people is the only thing that can solve your problem

Everyone who ever tries to go up the ladder, whether in business, politics, or what it may be, sooner or later finds that he must make himself known and "appreciated" by those beyond his regular sphere. What you want and need is a little different.

It isn't enough for you to be known and appreciated. You need more than that,—you need to have people beyond your regular sphere see, feel and be affected by your self power.

Publicity might solve the problem for those others, but it can't solve your problem. Publicity is a technique for advertising and selling to people something they might not otherwise "see" or experience. What you need is more,—*you need to have people really see, feel and experience your self power* (not just hear of it).

For you then, only one thing can solve the problem,— exposure to more and more people. You don't need publicity techniques, you need *exposure* techniques.

4. The exposure techniques

There are dozens of different exposure techniques, but many are usable only in certain fields and a few others apply only to special social or economic situations. However, there are three key ones that apply for you no matter what the instance or circumstance.

The three keys to greater exposure of your self power can be labeled "circulate," "travel," and "vary." If you will stay alively conscious of their importance and what each of them calls for, the vigor of your self power will build constantly and its effectiveness will never wane.

5. Vary those of your habitual doings that involve contacts

Whether you are in a business, a profession, or in politics, you have a number of fixed contacts (or exposures) that continue day after day and that you can't change. These are your family, your associates, and your customers, clients, parishioners, or whatever. However, you also have some fixed contacts you can change or vary, ones that are fixed only because habit or something else has made them so.

Like everyone else, you see certain advantages in eating, drinking, shopping, etc., in the where-you-are-known places. Through habit (or some reason of preference) you eat lunch regularly in the same one or two places and just as regularly try to have the same waiters or waitresses serve you. If you patronize bars or cocktail lounges, the same forms of habit or preference again guide you. And, as you buy clothing, groceries, or do any other shopping, again either habit or some preference guides you to the same places again and again. It even extends to your haircuts, shoe shines, and to your magazine and newspaper buying.

In the doing of all of these things, your habits or preferences have resulted in fixed contacts and thus limited your sphere. It's something you can't let be. You can't afford to limit your sphere, therefor you can't afford fixed contacts in things when they can be varied.

6. As you build the vigor of your self power, you build yourself too

Regardless of how great the advantages are in doing business with the where-you-are-known places (and it cannot be denied that those advantages can be great ones), when you are a self power the disadvantages outweigh the advantages. In other words, the advantages you will gain from wider exposure far outweigh the greatest advantages of concentrating on the where-you-are-known places.

As your first move then toward increasing your exposure for the building of your self power's vigor, begin immediately to vary more in your regular doings. When you go to lunch tomorrow, go somewhere you've never tried before. (If you are the self power you should be by now, the instant you walk into the new place your self power will bring you attention and service equal to the best your customary eating places ever give you. If it doesn't, then you haven't heeded the hints and techniques that have been given you and, as a consequence, haven't built your self power to what it should be by now.) Later in the week try another restaurant. And next week try two or three more.

Vary your other shopping the same way. Whether you currently need new sox or ties, go look at some tomorrow in a store that is new to you. For your next hair trim, go to a different barber shop. Get your shoe shine from a different bootblack tomorrow. And pick up your newspaper from a different newstand, buy your cigars at a different tobacco counter, and purchase some toothpaste or aspirin at a different drug store.

These are only a few of your customary doings that you can and should vary. If you customarily make the weekly grocery shopping trip with your wife, take her to a different store this week. On the way, buy your gasoline at a different service station. Drop your suits off at a different cleaners. Stop in at a different bakery. And top it all off by buying her that usual weekly gift of candy or flowers from a shop that doesn't know you.

Extend the varying of your exposure to everything you possibly can. Each new person you expose yourself to is one more person who will see, feel and be affected by your self power. Each of them will definitely and consciously notice you and be aware of you. And then, as they see you from time to time, they'll remark to others about you,—and as they remark about you to others, their remarks will increasingly reach to your fixed contacts. *Every one of these remarks that reaches your fixed contacts is a boost.* It shows your sphere as bigger and bigger, it shows your power as going farther and farther beyond those close to you, and it thus supplies more and more vigor to your self power and keeps it from stagnating and waning. And in the meantime, it builds you, too.

7. Circulate outside your prescribed or customary contact areas

Your second move in the increasing of your exposure to build your self power's vigor should be aimed at the fixed contacts you can't vary. This means those persons who are primarily associates, friends, neighbors, customers and such, persons with whom your contact is brought about by your work plus your home life and location (and who would thus only change if you changed jobs or moved to a new area).

Since these contacts can't be varied (and your exposure increased in that manner), the best way to increase your exposure here is to circulate wider. By this is meant, make your customary contact areas broader and keep extending them.

8. Circulate to expose yourself to people, not to court them

How you broaden your contact areas concerned with your work will depend a lot on your actual job. For example: If you are a supervisor or manager of a section or department, your first move would be to make a practice of circulating in other sections or departments by visiting them as frequently as possible and thus exposing yourself (and your self power) to the people in them. If you are the head of a business, your first move would be to make a practice of circulating in other kindred businesses by visiting them as frequently as possible so as to expose yourself (and your self power) to the people in these kindred businesses. If you are a clergyman, your first move would be to make a practice of visiting other congregations as frequently as possible to expose yourself (and your self power) to the people in as many congregations as possible.

No matter what your job, your first move should be to circulate with increasing frequency in more and more parallels of your own customary contact area. The more you expose yourself and your self power to the people in them, the more vigor will your self power have in your *customary* contact area.

This same applies where neighbors and friends are concerned. So, instead of exchanging greetings with only your immediate neighbors, start nodding recognizingly to those neighbors beyond them and exchange greetings more widely. *However, remember that you are on the self power path, not the good fellow path; do not try to extend your exposure by entertaining more, by being a "joiner," nor even by accepting more invitations.* Confine yourself strictly to exposure; let others see you and see you as approachable (your bars down), but do not court them; if they show their arms as open to you, show yourself as appreciative but don't rush into them. As pointed out in earlier chapters, no matter how much others open for you, never move toward them, always let them move toward you.

9. Travel outside the areas where you are known

Travel always does many things for you or any of us. In this instance, though, all those usual things are secondary. You are interested in travel here only as a means of increasing your exposure.

With regard to the importance of increasing your exposure, Alfred E. Smith had this to say approximately a decade after his defeat for the Presidency: "Though prejudice and a lot of other things had a lot to do with it (his defeat), the big thing was lack of exposure. If through the years I'd exposed myself more in other areas instead of identifying myself so strongly with only one area, a lot of the prejudice and other things wouldn't have existed."

And the former president of one of our major industries had the following to say about exposure: "I never became a real power because I didn't use the same common sense with regard to myself that I did with our marketing. Whether it's yourself or a product, and no matter how much self power, quality or merit you or it has, the only thing that can build its vigor and keep it on the increase is an ever widening exposure of it."

Use travel as a means for adding to the exposure of your self power. Whatever your area now is (the one in which you live, work and are recognized), travel a little beyond it at every opportunity. But as you do it, *expose yourself to people.*

When you set out to expose yourself to people, don't just ride through an area, whether it is another section of town, an adjoining town, or a farm community. Stop and expose yourself everywhere you can. Whether you buy only cigarettes, a candy bar, a sandwich, a handkerchief, or some other small item, use your small purchases as an excuse to go into and expose yourself in as many places as possible. Your self power will be seen and felt in all of them. And because of it, the people who talk to you or just see you will wonder about you and ask each other (or even you) who you are. However, with or without the answer, *they'll remember you,* and sooner or later identify you.

Tiny and time-wasting as all these things may now seem to you as you do them, it will only be a short while until you begin to experience how much they are building your self power's vigor. Take a tip from the combined and condensed advice of some outstanding self powers: Once you've built your self power there is nothing more important to it than the building of its vigor; *put at least as much ingenuity to work toward increasing the exposure of your self power as you do toward earning a living.*

10. Points worth special attention

1. Never recognize or accept any limits on your self power.

2. The self power you already have built is the only equipment you need to push it beyond all limits.

3. Once you are a self power, the vigor of your self power is built by the quantity of people who see, feel and are affected by it.

4. Exposure of your self power, not publicity of it, is the thing that makes it seen and felt.

5. Varying your habitual doings that involve contacts is the first key to building your self power's vigor.

6. Extend the varying to everything you can, even to the smallest of doings like shoe shines and newspaper purchases.

7. Circulating outside your customary contact areas is the second important key to building your self power's vigor.

8. Travel outside the areas in which you are known is the third important key to building your self power's vigor.

9. Remember, you vary, circulate and travel to expose your self power to people, not to court them.

10. Remember also, once you have built your self power, nothing is more important to it than the building of its vigor.

11. Put as much ingenuity into increasing your self power's exposure as you do into earning a living, for the more ingenuity you put into the exposure, the greater your self power's vigor.

16

HOW TO ACHIEVE AND MAINTAIN MAXIMUM POWER EFFECTIVENESS

The higher you ascend the more you need to delegate responsibility for detail and supervision to helpers.

A self power's helpers must be genuine assistants or lieutenants, not "skills" hired to do a job.

The skill and knowledge of your helpers is of only secondary importance.

Pull your helpers by opening opportunity to them, not by "buying" them.

There are right and wrong ways to open opportunity.

The "show me" technique strengthens your pull on those who venerate and believe in you.

With the "show me" technique, you maintain maximum effectiveness and never surrender or dilute your power, influence or control.

Spreading your power and building its vigor will be a big factor in your rising to higher levels. Your advance to higher levels, and to their greater responsibilities, brings you new problems however. One of these is the achieving and maintaining of maximum effectiveness as you increasingly need to delegate responsibility to others.

162

1. To maintain maximum self power effectiveness, you must use different standards in delegating responsibility

Several times in your climb to self power you have had to coldly and realistically face facts and recognize that the self power path has nothing in common with the fellowship path, with the ordinary so-called "personal" power paths (which are really agency power and buying power), or with any other path. You have had to face the fact that none of those others (in even the tiniest degree) can be mixed with your self power, that mixing them in your self power dilutes and destroys it.

Now you are going to have to face those facts coldly and realistically again. You need to recognize that, when you are a self power, you must use different standards and methods in delegating responsibility to others if you are to achieve and maintain maximum self power effectiveness.

2. You need helpers, but you can't afford to "buy" them as others do

When you rise to higher and higher levels (in business, politics, or any other endeavor), whether you get there by self power or any other means, you find it necessary to have assistants, lieutenants, or some other form of helpers. In other words, no matter how great a power you become, you aren't a superbeing; time itself puts limitations on the amount of detail and supervision you unassistedly can take care of. As a consequence, and whether you want to or not, when you move higher you need to delegate more and more responsibility for detail and supervision to helpers.

The man who isn't a self power faces but one basic consideration in deciding on any helper and it is no different than that he faces in hiring any other underling: Who is the person best qualified and equipped to handle the detail or supervisory task concerned? With the decision made, he sets about the hiring of that person. His only problem is how much (in money, titles, side benefits, bonuses, etc.) it will take to entice (buy) that person's services.

Your problem is less simple. In your case (though you too hire regular underlings on that basis) the considerations and problem are different when you seek assistants. As a self power, you can't afford to select and acquire helpers in the same manner that you acquire skills. As a self power you are forced to recognize that you can hire and buy skills "to do a job," but you can't hire or buy the main ingredient that must be in any persons you are to entrust with being genuine assistants or lieutenants.

3. Your only problem is that of laying opportunity open to people

Because you are a self power, when you select any helper your basic consideration cannot be who is best qualified and equipped. To you, the skill of your helpers must be second in importance to another consideration. Instead of looking first at who is qualified and equipped, you must look first at *who are the persons most affected by* (and thus most partisan to) *your self power*. Those are the persons who put you and your interests first and themselves and their interests second, seeing their interests as common with and linked to your own.

This means persons who are genuinely partisans of yours. It does not mean persons who "hitch their wagons to yours" to use you for purposes of their own. As warned in Chapter 14, you must learn to recognize and reject the "cooperation" of these. Nor does it mean persons you may sell on the idea of hitching their wagon to yours. Again, and as warned in Chapter 14, no matter how much other kinds of powers engage in that practice, you can't afford to.

With the decision made as to who are most affected by your self power, your next consideration is that of which among them may be qualified or equipped, *or is trainable,* to handle the detail and supervision concerned. Once you have decided who these persons are, your problem of acquiring them as helpers becomes relatively simple. It involves nothing more than a proper means of opening the opportunity to them. Remember though, *not the offering of opportunity as a bribe to them;* merely the opening to them of the opportunity to be assistants of yours.

4. Make the other feel complimented that opportunity is put within his reach

There are right and wrong ways to lay open the opportunity for another to be an assistant of yours. If you do it the wrong way, you gain nothing,—the result in such instance is that the other is doing you a favor (by becoming your assistant) that is no less than the favor you did him (by offering him the opportunity).

Here are some of the wrong ways that are commonly used: (a) "I can use someone with your know-how (or ambition, knowledge, etc.); how would you like an opportunity as my assistant?" (b) "You're a good man and you deserve a chance at something better; how would you like an opportunity as my assistant?" (c) "I need another assistant and I've been looking for someone like you; how would you like a crack at it?"

To say any of those things, or any of the hundred others that parallel them, makes others see you as selfishly gratuitous, bestowing favors for selfish reasons. The person you say them to is no more complimented than the carpenter, chauffeur, cook, gardener or baby-sitter to whom you would say, "I've got a job for someone like you; how would you like to have a try at it?" As a result, the person will take the job, and maybe be happy to get it, but he'll look on you as having offered it to him because you need him, not because you were generous.

When you open opportunity, you must make it solely *opportunity proffered,* never a mere guise of opportunity. You must make the other feel complimented that you have put the opportunity within his reach. You must make him see the opportunity as one that could never be opened (or earned or merited) by the greatest of skill or knowledge qualifications: you must proffer it as something open only for one who is truly loyal and partisan to you. And the best means for doing that is the "show me" technique.

5. Persons not devoted to you and your interests are never genuine "helpers"

At whatever moment you first need to acquire helpers (persons to act and speak for you) you may be anywhere from the bottom to the top on the executive ladder. Regardless of where on it you are, whether you are a foreman, supervisor or manager of a small group, or are a corporation president, labor head, political head, or anyone else seeking assistants or lieutenants, you should use exactly the same means to select and pull your assistants and lieutenants.

In each instance, and at every level, you want these persons as genuine helpers, persons loyal to you and your interests, —as said, you want them to be something more than those persons you hire to do a job. Once again, these latter you can and should select because of their capability (skills) and the dependableness of their performance with it, but your helpers must be selected above all because they "worship and believe in you" and because of the dependableness of their loyalty to you and your interests (with their skill qualifications and trainability being but of second importance in the consideration).

One thing all self powers quickly learn: *It is far better to do without assistants and lieutenants than to ever acquire even one who is not genuinely devoted and loyal to you and your interests.* Bluntly, if among those who "worship and believe in you" there are none sufficiently qualified or trainable for the responsibility to be delegated, delegate it to no one; instead, continue to personally oversee all those who are answerable to you (whether these be individual workers, supervisors, or top executives) and accord none of them a status as "assistant" to you (let the status of each be clearly that of a person employed solely to do the job with which he is charged).

6. The "show me" technique

When you open opportunity to one you believe can genuinely be entrusted with the status of assistant to you, don't hand him the opportunity, only open it to him. For example: "I'll be needing an assistant soon, someone who can follow my thinking and speak and do exactly as I would myself on things. It's not easy, and not many people can push their own thinking aside and make themselves think and do like someone else,—but I was wondering if you might be able to."

Those are the exact words that many self powers use. Others vary them slightly but they never deviate from their pattern. Those words, few as they are, (a) show an opportunity as opening, (b) show it calls for someone "extra special," (c) show the obligation it entails, (d) show the opportunity as one to be regarded as an honor,—and they then (e) compliment the other by indicating consideration of him for the honor, (f) don't hand him the opportunity but put the opportunity open *so he can ask for it,* and (g) finally in effect say "if you want it and think you can fill the bill as that extra special someone, *show me!*"

The "show me" technique eliminates all the disadvantages of the "buying" approach and the selfishly gratuitous approach, and in addition has many hidden advantages. By those very means that it accomplishes the things just enumerated, it also accomplishes other things that are important to you:

One, it opens the opportunity to the chosen person *without making a definite job offer to him;* thus, by reason of your wording, if he passes up the opportunity he has not turned down a job you have offered,—instead, he has in effect considered himself not competent for nor worthy of an opportunity he could have asked for.

Second, it puts forth, as the prime qualification, that he push his own thinking aside and think and do only as you would; thus, the other is forced to be ever conscious that, regardless of other qualifications, he can continue as your assistant only so long as he abandons all exercise of individuality in the discharge of the responsibilities delegated to him.

7. The trick of the "show me" technique

The big trick of the "show me" technique lies in making your words lay open the opportunity challengingly while making the challenge a compliment ("—not many people can— but I was wondering if you might be able to—"). All of your words as you use the "show me" technique are important but those few are the most important to its success.

Brevity is the rest of the trick. If you prefer to use words of your own instead of those already being used by many self powers, at least make yours as brief as theirs are. And make yours as effective as theirs are. Make sure your words (1) name the opportunity, (2) specify it as for someone extra special, (3) indicate its obligation, (4) show it as an honor, (5) compliment the other through consideration of him, (6) lay the opportunity open so he can ask for it, and then (7) imply the big "show me."

8. The "show me" technique is your only sure means of maintaining maximum self power effectiveness

If you will use the "show me" technique in every instance where you need someone as an actual assistant or lieutenant, you will never have the problem of your power, influence or control being thinned as it spreads.

With the "show me" technique, your first move *always* is that of considering none for the job except those who "worship" you and believe in you,—and who believe that their own interests are best served by putting your interests first at all times. If you will look only to these persons as you set about the acquiring of assistants and lieutenants, and will use only the "show me" technique in opening the opportunity to any of them, you will never need to surrender any of your power, influence or control to others as you expand it and will, instead, be able to achieve and maintain a maximum effectiveness of it no matter how wide and deep you spread it.

But at this point the far spreading of your self power is not your only concern. As pointed out at the beginning of this chapter, you are rising to higher and higher levels and each of these brings you new problems. Maintaining maximum effectiveness as you spread and rise is the first of those problems, and though the "show me" technique solves it for you *at any level*, it can only solve it for you at the higher levels you achieve *if you make yourself rise to those levels as a person.*

As a consequence, you yourself must rise with your levels, and the doing of this is the second of the problems brought on by your increasing self power. Rise with your levels, as covered by the chapter that follows, and the "show me" technique will enable you to maintain maximum effectiveness *no matter how high you rise* as well as no matter how expansively you spread.

9. Points worth special attention

1. Genuine assistants or lieutenants can't be selected and hired on the basis all other underlings are.

2. You must select your helpers from among those persons most affected by your self power.

3. It is far better to do without assistants and lieutenants than to ever acquire even one who is not genuinely devoted and loyal to you and your interests.

4. Never hire or "buy" your helpers.

5. When you have selected whom you want as your helper, lay the opportunity open to him; don't hand him the opportunity.

6. Use the "show me" technique and never deviate from its seven points.

7. Your words must lay the opportunity open challengingly but make the challenge a compliment.

8. Brevity is essential to the technique's success.

9. When worded properly, as illustrated in section 6, two sentences can present and accomplish all the features enumerated at the end of section 7.

10. By never deviating from the "show me" technique in your acquiring of assistants, you assure you will never thin or surrender your power, influence or control and will maintain maximum effectiveness of your self power no matter how far you spread it.

17

HOW TO RISE WITH YOUR POWER LEVELS

Your power, influence and control is genuine only over those who genuinely accept you.

Your self power can elevate you but it alone can't win you acceptance.

You win acceptance only by fitting yourself into each environment you encounter.

Unless you "fit yourself in" the elements that make you a misfit will becloud your quality as an individual and self power.

The "dry run" technique is your surest means for knowing new environments and fitting yourself into them.

Your self power is elevating you at a fast pace. However, every "inch" it pushes you upward it also is pushing you farther beyond the people, customs, language, social graces and other things that have for so long been familiar. And, as it pushes you beyond them, it pushes you into areas (levels) where some of those heretofore familiar graces and things are inadequate and out of place. As a result, if you are to keep pace with your self power and be able to maintain your self power as it elevates you, you must at the same time and at the same rate make you yourself rise to the successively higher levels it carries you.

1. New areas and levels demand adjustments

If you will take time out now and assess yourself and your self power very critically three things will stand out.

One thing you should have seen by now is that the elevation your self power brings you comes very little from the mere having of self power; not your self power, but the constant redoing of those things you do to acquire and maintain self power, is what lifts you to higher levels. It lifts you there—quickly, easily and exhilaratingly—but it alone is never enough to keep you there!

And there is one thing more you should be seeing by now. Your self power, no matter how great it is, and though it is noticed by all people, has a controlling effect *only on those who see you at or beyond their own levels!*

These first two things make you see the third one: The more you progress with your self power, the more it demands that you elevate your personal self in every possible way! In other words, as your self power carries you to higher levels you *must* make your personal self rise with it to those levels or your self power melts away.

Thus, in addition to all other things the effectiveness of your self power is dependent on, it also is dependent on your ability to adjust and fit into new environments.

2. To "be and belong" requires greater changes than the ones you automatically make

When you began your acquiring of self power you began it among persons who were of a definite business or professional or political level. They (and your friends) were also of a definite language level, social level, economic level, interest level and mental perspective level. And those levels were your levels too at that time.

Because those levels were your levels, you were familiar with the habits, customs, conversation, manners, deportment, standards and viewpoints prevailing at those levels. They were a major portion of your environment of the time and you were fully at ease and at home in that environment. However, immediately you began to fashion yourself into a self power, you elevated yourself automatically a little beyond your familiar level (and all those persons in it)—and found yourself in new and strange environments.

As your self power has further increased you have moved on into higher and higher business or professional or political circles. And, with each tiny rise, you have found the habits, customs, conversation, manners, deportment, standards and viewpoints in these higher circles increasingly different from those that were familiar to you. As a result, you have, despite your self power, sometimes felt a little strange and not entirely "at home" as you first stepped to these higher levels,—*you have at the moment felt yourself on someone else's ground instead of on your own.*

To overcome this, to not be a stranger in these higher levels, and to exert your self power in them, you have found you have had to make some changes in your personal self. Don't deny it. You have had to quit being "yourself" and make alterations. Most specifically, you have had to try to alter certain of your manners, deportment and conversation to match what you've found prevailing in your new environments!

That in itself, no matter how little it has been, is a part of the process of making yourself rise with your levels. It's a start that gives recognition to the need for doing so, but it's nothing more than that. For you to "be and belong" at the successively higher levels requires much more change than just those little ones you or anyone makes automatically.

3. Unacceptability results more from customs and standards differences than from quality differences

Some persons who fashion themselves into self powers react strongly against the statement that they must alter their personal selves in order to successfully be and belong at the higher levels they achieve. They look on any such statement as telling them they aren't good enough for acceptance in new areas and at higher levels. If you are one of these, *you must either change your thinking now or be satisfied to forever be a limited self power*—whose power, influence and control is restricted to spreading only at your own and lower levels.

I recently sat by and listened to two hours of some "business and social graces" coaching that was being given to a new singing star. Two "sneak" recordings had rocketed him to the top and his manager and others were trying to prepare him for appearances at important functions, a tour, and various special engagements. Twice I heard him say, "But why can't I just be myself?" And both times his manager and the others told him, "Because it would put you right back where you started from and keep you there!"

To let yourself think as you should think, you must recognize that, no matter what your level now is (in business, politics, etc., or economically, socially, etc.), there are levels above you, aside from you and below you. You don't deny that the habits, manners, language, perspective, etc., of the levels below you are unacceptable to you in many respects; and you would be being hypocritical if you denied that these things made the persons of those levels unacceptable at your own level. For the same reasons (*and not because of "who is better than who"*) you must recognize that you cannot be or belong at the levels you rise to unless you make your own personal habits, manners, language, etc., rise to those of these higher levels also.

4. Preliminary observation of new environments is a precaution your common sense dictates

Once the chip is off your shoulder, what do you need to do to make your personal self rise to the levels you are carried to by your self power? First of all, you need to be exceedingly observant. In order to know what is acceptable in any area or level (in those things we call the business and social graces and language) you must know what prevails there. This is just as important in your rise to new levels as it is in your travel to new places.

A self power in the business machines field points to it this way: When he was small his family moved quite often, but always to better and better neighborhoods. His mother, however, never took their acceptance for granted and took great pains to "belong" wherever they went. When they moved to a new neighborhood she made him and his brothers watch the other children (from a window) for two or three days before going out to play with them. When the family went to a new church she herded them into a back pew the first Sunday or two. And when they went to any house a first time for lunch or dinner she made them put observation ahead of eating. He says, "It was her way of forcing us into a habit of being attentive to new environments so we wouldn't do even any little thing that might be unacceptable and cause us not to belong."

His comment on it: "We boys looked on our being temporarily held back from play, eating, and lots of other things, as a punishment, but the observation habits she built in us have guarded me from self embarrassment time and time again. Not only that, they have saved me from being a misfit in any of the many levels I've passed through in rising from the shops to where I am. To her, that scouting kind of observation of new environments was nothing more than *a precaution dictated by common sense,*—and even when it's called the 'dry run' technique, it's still nothing more than that."

5. The "dry run" technique

That last sentence in the preceding paragraph pretty well sums the "dry run" technique. It is "a scouting kind of observation" of every new environment you encounter. And, as that sentence also points out, such scouting observation really is nothing more than a precaution your own common sense should dictate.

Whenever you enter a new area (whether it is a place that is new, or is a new group of people, or is a new level of business, society, or anything else), do as that mother made her children do. No matter what the circumstances are that put you there, and even if you are an honored guest or the main attraction, *do nothing* (other than smile and nod pleasantly) until you have fully observed what is customary for that area, group or level. Let your first entries into each of the new environments be a dry run, a scouting mission, devoted entirely to observing every little thing that is in any way different.

You don't have to worry about the big things. The big things (in manner, deportment, customs, etc.) stand out and come to your attention at once. Those are ones you and all sensitive people adjust to automatically. Your concern is with the little things (*which stick out as big things* if you do ignore them).

The little things may be anything from how to shake hands to how to sit at a meeting or dinner table, or from when to rise or sit to what tone to converse in. They may pertain to how to walk or how to dress (what you wear and how much or how little, of clothing, jewelry and accessories). No one, not even a book on etiquette or the graces, can give you the answers; what is fixedly decorous in one instance or group or place is unseemly or unfitting in others. As a consequence, your only sure way to get the answers (toward avoiding self embarrassments and faux pas) is by using the "dry run" technique.

6. The tricks of the technique are the rules that govern it

Success of the "dry run" technique, and your success with rising with your levels, depends on two simple things that all people (and especially powers) find difficult. These are spoken of as the tricks of the technique but in reality they are the rules for it.

The first of these has already been mentioned. On your first entry into or encounter with any new area, *do and say nothing* beyond any absolute minimum that is definitely and pointedly required of you. Make your first encounter a "dry run." Use it as a scouting mission and observe every detail of what show as prevailing customs, courtesies, deportment, language and all else that in any manner is different.

The second trick or rule goes hand in hand with the first but is even more difficult for most people to follow. It calls for you to deliberately hang back on your "dry run." Let others sit or stand first, eat or drink first, greet or take leave first, etc. That is, let others make the first move on everything and let them initiate and carry all conversation so that you may observe what customs prevail before you do or say anything. In short, don't take the lead in anything, not even in asking a question, expressing an opinion, accepting a cocktail, smoking, unfolding a napkin, or any of the hundred other things you normally would not reflect on before doing.

7. Genuine power, influence and control is possible only over those who accord you genuine acceptance

None of what is set forth means that you are to abandon your self power or self power attitude in any way whatever. You are a self power and you must remain one,—but during your "dry runs" you must assume the role of a "spectator" self power and not let yourself be drawn into being a performer. And when you are in the center of things, particularly as the honored guest or main attraction, this is more important than ever. All eyes are on you more critically at such a time and nothing that could mark you as not belonging escapes them.

The problem of making yourself rise with your levels may be more real than you like to admit but you cannot ignore it.

Again, it is not one of making yourself "as good as" someone else,—it is simply one of carefully fitting yourself into new environments so that *the measure of you* (by those in them) *will be made solely on your quality as an individual and self power,* and not on the basis of any inharmoniousness of customs, manners, language, deportment, courtesies, perspective, or the like.

Your self power can elevate you to any level and take you into any area. It's a vehicle that can take you anywhere you want to go. But, no matter how great it is, it alone is not enough to fit you in and make you belong in any of the places to which it takes you. The more you are attentive to this and use the "dry run" technique, the faster you'll find genuine acceptance and the greater will your power, influence and control be among all people at all levels and in all areas.

Some people only learn the hard way. Don't ever be one of them,—too often experience gives you knowledge only when it is too late to use it. Until you are in a position where there are no environments beyond you or your experience, open your eyes to reality and give proper recognition to the fact that genuine power, influence and control is possible only over those who accord you genuine acceptance!

8. Points worth special attention

1. If you are to maintain your self power as it elevates you, you must at the same time and same rate elevate your personal self.

2. Your self power has a controlling effect only on those who see you at or beyond their own levels.

3. You can't carry the elements of one environment into another; you must abandon the old and adjust to the new.

4. Only observation can with any certainty acquaint you with the customs, manners, deportment, language, and other distinctive factors of any environment.

5. Make your first entries into any new area, group or level strictly a scouting mission, regardless of the circumstances.

6. Use the "dry run" technique to avoid self embarrassments and the faux pas that would mark you as "not belonging."

7. Until you have carefully observed what the customs, manners, language, etc., of an environment are:

8. Do and say nothing beyond any absolute minimum required of you, and

9. In the meantime, let others make the first move on everything and let them initiate and carry all conversation.

10. Don't subdue your self power, however; put it forth as strongly as ever but be a "spectator" self power.

18

HOW TO WIN IN A POWER DUEL

> Agency powers, being only wielders of power, feel their inferiority and recognize their insecurity.
>
> Agency powers see you and all self power as a force they must combat.
>
> The standoff-standout technique disposes of those who try the show-of-power game.
>
> The rubber skin technique disposes of those who thrust at you from above.
>
> The dog-bone technique disposes of those who attack solely through jealousy.
>
> Other than pressure, agency powers have no techniques or weapons.

You aren't the only person who is seeking to build his power, influence and control over people. The higher and wider your self power carries you, the more of these others you will meet. You will find them everywhere and, whether you wish it or not, and despite any efforts on your part to avoid it, a power duel will develop with many of them. When it does, you can't bow out of it or back away from it. And you don't dare come away from it with less than a stalemate.

1. Let your self power assert itself; don't try to wield it

On the whole, the only "powers" who will try to assert their superiority are false powers (agency powers, etc., as set forth in section 7 of Chapter 2 and section 3 of Chapter 14). As mentioned earlier, no matter what front or bravado they display, such powers always know within themselves that they only wield power and aren't powers themselves. As a consequence, they constantly fear the self power, seeing him always as something they must combat (no matter how unpushing he is) in order to preserve their own "power" in any area. These fearful false powers are the only "powers" who are your problem.

By contrast, the self powers who try to assert their superiority are never a problem to you. The few of these you will meet will be only partial self powers, ones who have not yet developed fully into self powers and who therefor are less self assured than you are. Their attempts at exerting their superiority will always be seen by all as an envious grab toward it and will thus serve only to emphasize their lack of it.

2. The standoff-standout technique

What has just been said gives you your first key to winning in a power duel. Namely, never try to display your superiority. Merely let what self power you have assert itself and you will always be seen as superior to those who try to wield or make a show of power. When you are deliberately a standoff from the show-of-power game, you are always more a standout and winner (to spectators and participants both) than any show of power could make you.

The smaller show-of-power games are going on about you all the time. Maybe you haven't in the past seen them as what they are, but from here on you must. Every time someone makes a show of (or brags of) the service or compliance he gets from tradespeople, employees, or anyone else, recognize it as an attempt to draw you into a power duel. And then do nothing, other than to maintain your self power at its fullest.

The standoff-standout technique is that and nothing more. However, though it is a do-nothing technique and the simplest of all, most people find it difficult,—simply because they can't resist the tendency to vie with those who brag of or display power. If you are one of these, break yourself of that tendency at once. No challenge is worth taking up that is going to necessitate the forfeiture of your self power.

3. Self power is the only power that people truly honor and respect

Power duels (between self powers and agency powers) have always been given prominence in history, mythology, religious literature and instructive anecdotes. They are scattered through the Bible, the Koran, the Zend-Avesta, the Vedas, and all other holy books, and through the folklore, mythology and legends of every land and race. They are similarly prominent in almost every biography, whether it be of a Lincoln, a Napoleon or a Schwab. Wherever you come across a person, real or imaginary, who is pictured as an unusually great figure, you are almost certain to find power duels ascribed to him and to find him pictured as a self power (whether he was or not) emerging victorious over all forms of false power.

Those things in themselves are interesting, if for no other reason than that they point out that the qualities of self power have been recognized for thirty or forty centuries. For you, however, it all has a special interest at this time. It shows you how the minds of people through the many centuries have honored and respected self power while showing a disdain and lack of sympathy toward all other power.

4. The power duels of history and legend supply extra tips on winning

Seemingly without exception the power duels of history and legend show one pattern. They show the false power as trying to provoke the self power into a wielding of power (knowing that only the wielding of it can weaken it), and then show the false power as thwarted and defeated when the self power continues on with being steadfastly a self power instead of reducing himself to power wielding.

That pattern is an accurate one and you will find it applying to every duel. In each instance, the person with agency power who wants to make a show of superiority will try to provoke you into a wielding of power. *If he succeeds, you cease to be a power and instead become, like him, but a power agent.* Your winning in every instance depends on your abstaining from wielding power and continuing unshakenly to exercise solely your self power.

No matter how little attention you have paid to the power duels of history and legend in the past, from here on scrutinize them carefully as you come across them. None of them are perfect, but every one of them will supply you with added tips on the maintaining of your self power when false powers attack it.

5. False powers are desperate powers

Power duels occur for one reason. Though other things may add to the reason for them, *the only reason power duels occur is because another "power" sees himself at his maximum, knows he cannot step above or beyond you, and therefor tries to reduce you* (the only means he sees for being ahead of you)

Psychologists offer a variety of explanations for the actions of the false "power" but the best illustration of it is one Kaiser Wilhelm II gave more than half a century ago. Reduced to the fewest words it is as follows:

A false power is an armless man on a mountain ledge. He's there only because some agency put him there. He's unequipped to have climbed to that level himself and he can't climb above it, and he is therefor hatingly envious of all who can climb. As a consequence, *he does everything he can to keep others from reaching his ledge and going beyond him.* When any climber gets a fingerhold on his ledge he stomps on the climber's fingers.

If the climber manages to get onto the ledge, he tries to kick the climber off. And if he can't kick the climber off and the climber proceeds to climb above the ledge, he tries to bite at the climber's backside and heels to drag him back! Whether he uses trickery or outright force, he's the worst obstacle any with climbing ability and power encounters,—and the only way to get past him is to wear a shell of armor that his stomping and kicking and biting and trickery can't penetrate!

The Kaiser went on to explain that your shell can't be one you hide in, like a turtle or clam; it must be like a crab or lobster shell, one that lets you go on being yourself and doing as you would do.

6. There are no bounds to the viciousness of desperate powers

The illustration just recounted points up a type of power duelist somewhat different from those who merely play the show-of-power game. It shows a duelist who actually attacks you and your power, one who "does everything he can to keep you from reaching his level and going beyond him." In other words, he isn't someone competitive at your own level (like the show-of-power challengers), he is someone still above you, someone you have yet to reach and pass.

Let's take a look at who this attacking duelist might be. He (or she) might be an executive above you who has lost (or has no reason for) confidence in himself and recognizes that he can't advance beyond where he is. He might be a political or other figure who recognizes he has gone stale and is slipping. Or he may be an educator, a social personage, a performer, or anyone else who fears he couldn't cope with competition.

When the attacking duelist is any of those, he is desperate, as the illustration well describes. If he is an executive above you for example, he is likely to find fault with you when no fault exists, to countermand your instructions even when they are the very ones he himself directed, and most probably (behind your back) will make false complaints against you or even spread disparaging rumors. His tactics won't be fair and they will be aimed at getting rid of (you or anyone else) whoever might displace or surpass him.

When these things or their parallels happen, cowering before them or running from them will let the duelist accomplish his ends. Similarly, letting yourself be drawn into fighting them most often will serve his ends (being above you he has the advantage and can usually turn things about to show the antagonism as originating with you). As a consequence, your one sure way of winning is through use of the rubber skin technique.

7. The rubber skin technique

Where a duelist is baiting you, figuratively or actually daring you to pit your power wielding against his own, the standoff-standout technique is all you need. However, where a duelist is cutting and slashing at you, not just baiting you, you have no opportunity to be a standoff. Instead, you must stand your ground, not stand off, but do it with a rubber skin that can't be penetrated and that bounces back every thrust.

As an example: Don't at any time show that you feel any thrust or that any of them ruffle you. In other words, let nothing in your attitude or actions change. At the same time, don't be merely passively resistant. When unwarranted fault is found, show no antagonism but promptly say, "As you wish, but we both know you are wrong." When instructions are countermanded after you have been directed to issue them, say boldly, "You're losing face and prestige by countermanding yourself." And if any behind-the-back false complaints or rumor reach you, put your informant (whether a superior or underling) in front of your duelist and without heat say to your duelist 'Tell this man you're a liar."

That is strong bouncing back of the duelist's thrusts, but anything less strong would only serve to let him accomplish his purpose.

8. Never let yourself be tricked into using the other person's technique

If you have the necessary rubber skin or "shell,"—that is, a will strong enough to continue being a self power,—you have everything you need to win in any power duel.

As a self power you must always be conscious of the big difference people see between you and the false powers. That is something that works in your favor constantly. Agency power, even when it is only buying power, is always a weight that *presses* people (directly or indirectly) into compliance, cooperation, or other action. It blankets and weighs on people. Self power, on the other hand, is never a weight. It is like a pole that is pushing up on the blanket, taking the weight off. And, because it is, and because people see it so, people gravitate to it (where the weight is least) and help to push it higher.

Any "power" who attempts to show his superiority will always do so by showing how much weight he can put on people and will try to cause you to do the same. Weight is the only technique such a power has. Leave it to him and ignore it. The more weight he exerts, the more will people gravitate toward you where the weight is least!

In other words, the harder an agency power tries to win in a power duel, the greater he makes your victory,—providing you avoid his technique entirely and hold to being solely a self power.

9. Make the strength of your self power your offensive

What has been pointed out here with regard to power duels serves to explain why self powers are a greater rarity in politics than in any other field. Politicians rarely are able to see anything as ignorable. They see everything as something that must be countered, either by counteraction, countercharge or defense.

When you take any of those actions you automatically forfeit your self power. In winning power duels, you must let all the effort and action be put forth by those who want to show their superiority. And in doing this, you must never become defensive. Bounce the attacking duelist's thrusts but do nothing more. Again and again remind yourself, *your only counteraction must be a steady and unchanging continuance of your self power, its attitude and its techniques.* (Situations that are not power duels but are ones where attempts are made to put you on the defensive, etc., have already been dealt with in other chapters.)

All the pointers that can be given with regard to winning a power duel can be condensed into these four: (1) Don't ignore the person or his purposes; be very alert to both. (2) At the same time, ignore his every attempt toward forcing you *or tricking you* into pressing your power. (3) *Don't deviate a particle from being a self power* and, as such, put your efforts only into making yourself a better one than ever before. (4) Recognize your self power as your best offensive and one the false power can't parry; convince yourself that that is why he tries to trick or force you into abandoning it.

10. Jealousies always exist; handle them as you would the power duels

What applies to the handling of power duels also applies to the handling of out and out power jealousies.

The regular power duel occurs when a person, equal or higher in a path parallel to your own, tries to show his "power" superiority in order to lessen your status (administratively, socially, politically, or otherwise). In the out and out power jealousies the circumstance is somewhat different. In these some person tries to lessen your status simply because he is jealous of your power, not because you parallel him and may pass him.

For example: On an army post (during the last war) there were some outstanding self powers who had refused commissions. These men were deferred to and liked by everyone, including all of the commissioned personnel, except the commanding general. This latter, who was strictly an agency power, was jealous of the self power of these men from the first day he saw them. They were no threat to his power, were not even interested in military careers, but he was so jealous of their self power he resorted even to petty little things in his attempts to lessen their power status.

You may encounter this kind of power jealousy anywhere. You may be a businessman and find a politician or educator jealous of your self power. You may be in any field at all and still find dissociated persons in your own or any other field jealous of your self power.

11. The dog-bone technique

Whenever such a situation occurs, be conscious of it,—don't foolishly pretend it doesn't exist,—but ignore every attempt the other makes to show his superiority and go right on being the self power of which he is jealous. In ordinary instances handle him exactly as you would the one who tries to engage you in a power duel and he will soon make himself ridiculous. In more extreme instances (with vicious instead of petty displays of jealousy), use the dog-bone technique.

The dog-bone technique is exactly what its name indicates, —the throwing of a bone to a fractious dog. It's one of the favorites in the bag of tricks of greater self powers and they never hesitate nor delay in their use of it.

Circumstances will themselves determine what the "bone" should be. Most often though it is a forthright invitation to dinner or to some other somewhat private function or occurrence (such as a quite private preview of a new product, a new art purchase, etc.).

The trick of success of the dog-bone technique lies in two

small but important details. First, the invitation (or whatever is extended) must be extended forthrightly. Second, the function or occurrence must be a somewhat private one. This last is extremely important. An invitation to anything that is of party proportions would never be snatched at as a bone,—instead it would be (even if accepted) disdained as a crumb! And of course defeat the purpose.

12. Your "shell" and your self power are the only weapons you need

You or any man who is truly a self power has nothing to fear from power duelists or the power jealous. Very frankly, it is only while you are building yourself that the pointers given here are of first importance to you. *Once you have made yourself solidly a self power and have acquired the assurance that only self powers ever experience, nothing will ever ruffle you.* Your "shell" will be as much a part of your self power as all else that combines to make you one.

As a final pointer: Don't try tricks or other things as some would-be self powers have in the combatting of the duelists and the jealous. You don't need such things and they always work against you. Your "shell," your self power, and the three simple techniques for making best use of them are the only weapons you need. With them you can win every duel and defeat every jealousy, no matter what form either may take.

13. Points worth special attention

1. False powers, not other self powers, are your problem.
2. Use the standoff-standout technique to dispose of those who try the show-of-power game.
3. There is monumental proof that people respect self power but disdain and are unsympathetic toward all other power.
4. Pressure is the only weapon of the false powers.
5. The more weight you let false powers press with, the more will people gravitate toward you.
6. See the false power as a desperate and armless man on a ledge.

7. Use the rubber skin technique when false powers get desperate and attack.

8. Never be tricked into using agency power tactics.

9. Recognize and be conscious of jealousies; don't foolishly underestimate them or pretend they don't exist.

10. Use the dog-bone technique to dispose of the jealous attackers.

11. Your self power is an advantage no others can match.

12. With your shell, your self power, and the three simple techniques for making best use of them, you have all you need to win every power duel and defeat every jealousy.

19

HOW TO HANDLE DIFFICULT PEOPLE

Among the worst blights on society are those who get a
brutish satisfaction from demeaning others.

The tramplers, those with authority over you who try to
trample you are among the worst and must be stopped
on their first try.

Beagles, the acquaintances and strangers who impose on
your kindness and graciousness solely to demean you,
have a contempt for kindness and must be dealt with
roughly.

Whether a beagle is using trampler tactics or the "drop
something," "lose something," "helpless" or other tricks,
the objective is to show you as soft and weaker than he is.

Woodspussies, those who try to blacken or downgrade you
with a rumor stench, can and must be frustrated.

The secret of handling difficult people lies mostly in having
the "guts" to do so.

As Chapters 8 through 18 have pointed out, when you become a self power more and more people constantly gravitate
toward you but at the same time more and more people become
envious of you. Most of these try to in little or big ways show
themselves as equal or superior to you, and through the mentioned chapters you have been given the techniques for dealing

191

with them. Worse than any of these though, and more challenging of your self power, are the people who deliberately make themselves difficult (to you and all people) by trying to demean you and others for no reason other than a brutish satisfaction they get from doing so. They will try to demean anybody, but they put special effort forth in their trying to demean any who have popularity or power. Of all people, these are the most difficult.

1. The tramplers, the beagles and the woodspussies

People who get a brutish satisfaction out of demeaning others can be divided into three groups. One is composed of the tramplers, those who deliberately overstep their rights in trying to demean you. Another is made up of the beagles, those who use impositions (on your kindness, courtesy, etc.) to try to demean you. And the third is made up of the woodspussies, those (both individuals and organizations) who spread a stench of unfavorable gossip to try to demean you.

It is doubtful whether any self power would ever class any of these groups as less obnoxious than the others. All are blights on society and the most insidious and despicable of them are those who use innocence and mock politeness and gentleness while working their schemes. (Like the store manager who flips a coin to the assistant manager and says, "Get me a pack of cigarettes, will you?" He feigns an air that indicates he sees nothing wrong with his order or "request" but he deliberately has tried to cause the clerks and customers to see the assistant manager as only an errand boy.)

No matter how low your opinion is of tramplers, woodspussies and beagles, and despite how great your aversion to them might be, you can't avoid them. You'll encounter one or more of them in almost every group of people, whether it is a business, social, church, political, or any other kind of group. As a result, you must deal directly with them wherever possible and put them in the open whenever you come face to face with them.

2. Stop the trampler on his first try

The store manager just referred to is typical of the tramplers. You've met dozens of them. And, unless you have always been self-employed and have never had any executives above you, you are almost sure to have already had encounters with some of them. Here are some examples taken from the thousands of problem situations that climbing self powers have reported:

(a) An executive above you tosses you the keys to his car and says, "I had to park in a half hour zone; will you move my car before I get a ticket?" Or demeaning you doubly, he hands you some change and says, "Get me a cup of coffee, and get yourself one too." Or worse, and triply demeaning you, he tells his secretary to give you some money and have you go down to the drugstore to buy a new lipstick for his wife.

(b) In a meeting you are conducting, the executive above you interrupts and says, "You aren't getting the idea across; I'll explain it." Or, while he is talking, he tells you to erase the board for him, pick up the chalk for him, get some water for him, etc.

(c) While you are working hard with a client, the executive above you walks up to the client and says, "As soon as the simpler details are disposed of I'll go over the papers personally and take care of the fine points." Or, when you have dug up, developed and sold a new client, the executive above you introduces himself to the client and says, "You're the kind of client I feel should have my personal attention; if you'll come into my office I'll—"

Those few examples illustrate the most common tactics of the tramplers and probably have brought to your mind dozens of variations that you have observed or encountered. If you are generous, you may say that some tramplers trample thoughtlessly rather than intentionally. For your own sake, however, even while being generous, never let yourself be trampled. Once you let a trampler demean you he'll increase his efforts at it every time you try to stop him. *The only time it is easy to stop a trampler is the first time he tries to trample you.*

3. Never bristle; dish out the "treatment" calmly

Where a trampler is using the tactics illustrated in (a), the best way to stop him is to say, "I'll have someone do it." If his trampling does result from thoughtlessness, your words will point his thoughtlessness out to him and he'll apologize and either get someone else himself or thank you for doing so. In most instances, however, you will find the trampling is intentional and the reaction quite different.

The intentional trampler will feel rebuffed by your words. Most times he'll try to ignore them. In some instances (in order to hold command) he'll name a particular "someone" he wants to do the task. In other instances, though, he may even say, "I told *you* to do it." When this latter happens, he is deliberately trying to break you and menialize you, so you have nothing to lose in standing your ground. Pleasantly say, "And since being a servant or errand boy is outside my realm, I'm passing it on to one." He'll either give up or fire you, but he'll respect you (though maybe begrudgingly). Unless he is the owner of the business, however, the chances are very slim that he would dare fire you. If he does, though, you have lost far less than you would have had you bowed to him.

When the trampler is using the tactics illustrated in (b) and is trying to belittle you to those under your command, the best way to stop him is to nonchalantly give him some of his own medicine. For example, in the illustration used, after he has talked awhile, say politely, "I think it would be better if we put the point across differently; may I show you what I mean?" And then while you are talking, politely ask him to erase the board for you, hand you the chalk, etc. He may refuse, but he never again will try the same tactics on you.

When the trampler is using the tactics illustrated in (c) and is trying to minimize your importance, the best way to stop him is to reverse him. In an instance such as the first illustrated, tell him, "Because we saw the fine points as the most important, we've already taken care of them; would you like to check them with us before we go on to the simpler routine things?" Invariably that will stop him. In the other instance illustrated, break in on his comments and say to the client, "Go along and visit with him; now that everything is taken care of I don't want to waste your time by tying you up any longer." The inference won't be missed by either the client or the executive and both will have a higher regard for you.

If these "treatments" seem a little rough, remember they are far less so than the trampler is trying to be. Remember also, how successful you are with these "treatments" (or any variations) depends on how unruffled you remain. Thus, *the real trick in disposing of tramplers lies in not bristling and in dishing out the "treatment" with no change of manner.*

4. Beagles have a contempt for kindness

The beagles go side by side with the tramplers. However, they lack one advantage the trampler has (they have no authority over you) and as a result must resort to being either impositious or outright domineering in their attempts to demean you.

Like the tramplers, the beagles attack in various ways. Any beagle may use any means, but the beagle who is a "friend," a co-worker, a social acquaintance, a club associate, or the like, will most often use the same tactics indicated in the illustration (a) of the tramplers, trying to make you a servant or errand boy in any of a thousand ways. ("Take the golf clubs out to the car, will you?" "Go get us some drinks, will you?" "We're getting crowded; see if you can scare up some extra chairs, will you?"

Etc.) On the other hand, the beagle who is a stranger, though he or she may use those same tactics, more often will try to deftly trick or trap you into some act of politeness that can be construed as a serving of him and a demearing of yourself.

The beagle who resorts to trickery to maneuver you into serving him or her in some way is usually less directly impositious than the one who uses trampler tactics. Here are a few examples of the commoner tricks that are used every day by them, particularly on self powers and anyone of prominence:

(d) The "drop something" trick. It is one of the oldest, and though women are the biggest users of it, men of the beagle variety sometimes use it too. In one instance, while a prominent self power was signing a hotel register card, an expensively dressed and ambitious female rushed up to the hotel desk, fumbled in her handbag, and deliberately spilled its contents. In another instance, a male beagle loaded his arms high with books and folders and made a point of crossing the path of a prominent personage and cleverly spilling a small part of the load directly in front of him. Though the handbag and the overloaded arms are the commonest devices, the beagle who is set on making you serve him or her will drop anything from a diaper pin to a tiara.

(e) The "lose something" trick. This is a favorite with the beagle who catches you seated or standing still somewhere (in a train, a restaurant, a living room, or at your desk). The "loss," of course, is either deliberate or only pretended. The usual procedure is for the beagle to start searching around the area where you are seated. If you ignore the searching, the beagle will then mention the "loss" to you and say, "Do you see it anywhere?" Most often the item "lost" is either in earring, a wallet, a glove or cuff link, but it can be anything.

(f) The "helpless" trick. This one is the oldest of all, but new variations of it still show up every day. The beagles who employ it (male and female) can make themselves appear hopelessly helpless at anything from wielding a can opener to carrying an umbrella. They always pretend not to notice you as they go into their act but, if you ignore them, they make a to-do of their "helplessness" and ask you to come to their rescue.

(g) The "infirmity" trick. This is the one the determined beagle resorts to when the other tricks fail or don't seem appropriate. The beagle uses a fake faint (or "faintness"), a fake sprain, a pretense of a heart condition, or any of a thousand other momentary "infirmities" to cause you to serve him or her in some way.

These headings cover the most used tricks, but beagles are ingenious and they'll throw other tricks at you also. Sometimes their tricks are so professionally executed you may find it difficult to distinguish the trick drop, loss, helplessness or infirmity from the genuine. However, as was stated by one of the greatest self powers and the foremost scholar on the subject: *If you have the maturity and worldliness needed to be a self power, you can tell the difference between the trick and the genuine.*

The beagle is never the innocent he or she might seem. No matter whether the beagle is using trampler tactics or beagle tricks, the object of the beagle is to soften you. To the beagle, softness and pliableness, acts of courtesy or kindness, are a show of weakness. Whether he is male or female, he sees himself as stronger than you or your self power the instant you accommodate him. *He has a contempt for kindness,* and when you show him or her any kindness he transfers his contempt to you.

5. If you can't ignore a beagle, squelch him

When the beagle uses the trampler tactics, you can easily dispose of him (1) by using the same treatment on him you use on tramplers (where it is fitting) or (2) by ignoring him (just not hearing him) or (3) by saying to him, "That's something you can do better yourself." Wherever this last is your choice, make it a definite and final statement. Unless you do, the other will resort to persuasiveness and bring about a situation where you must either give in or be outstandingly rude.

When a beagle uses the "drop something" or any other beagle trick, the best thing always is to ignore him (or her). In the instances where you can't entirely ignore the beagle, the next best thing is to use a squelch. For example:

In the illustration of (d) the female beagle attracted the gentleman's attention to her spilled handbag and remarked on her own clumsiness. Instead of answering her or helping her, he turned back to the desk clerk and said, "I think the lady needs a porter and more practice."

In an instance where the "lose something" trick was pulled on a prominent professional man as he finished an interview, he ignored the request for help and said, "Our janitor is in charge of the lost and found department. My secretary will put you in touch with him."

In an instance where the "helpless" trick was tried on a high ranking political figure, the beagle walked up and stood beside him while he stood at the curb waiting for his car. She made a few dainty and timid gestures that no taxi driver could ever notice, then said to the political personage, "I just can't stop taxis; I need a whistle." When he continued to ignore her she said, "If you won't whistle for me I'll never get a taxi." Without turning to look at her he commented, "Raise your skirt high enough and you'll get taxis and whistles both."

6. Wade through the woodspussies; don't avoid them

The woodspussies present a quite different problem from those of the tramplers and beagles. The tramplers and beagles try to demean you when they are face to face with you but the woodspussies seldom do; in many cases they fawn over you when they face you and then do their demeaning behind your back.

The tramplers and beagles both try to demean you through trying to menialize you in one manner or another, but the woodspussies try to demean you by spreading gossip and rumors that will blacken your reputation or downgrade your accomplishments or abilities.

Because the woodspussies seldom disclose their activities to you, for the most part they feel secure from you. They know you have no way to call them to account and they also know that if you try to defend yourself against the stench they spread you make it more damaging to yourself.

Like with the woodspussies of the forest, the only way to combat and defeat them is to frustrate them; instead of avoiding them, be impervious to their stench so you can ignore it and wade right through them. Nothing so confuses and defeats them as does your deliberate non-avoidance of them. Whether you encounter them in social groups, in business, in church, or in a supermarket, deliberately put yourself among them,—and make them themselves do any avoiding that is to be done. The discomfort you provoke in them usually will rid you of them.

7. The secret of handling people is in having the "guts" to do so

Every self power admits that many people are deliberately difficult and that the greater your self power becomes the more of them you encounter. However, as most self powers point out, as your assurance increases and you see people more realistically, the handling of difficult people becomes routine and simple. In emphasis of this, one self power reduced it all to a single word. When asked what his real secret was for his success in dealing with the difficult or hard to handle people, he replied, "Guts!"

That one word answer is the key you need. Underscore it heavily and put it in the front of your mind. It means: *Have the guts to trample on tramplers and not worry about your job.*

Have the guts to ignore, trample on or squelch beagles and not worry that you might become unpopular with them. Have the guts to wade in among woodspussies and ignore their stench.

When you have the guts for all those things, your stature will mount and mount and put you above and beyond the reach of everyone. That, of one fashion or another, is what you are seeking or you wouldn't be striving to be a self power.

No matter how you analyze what you are seeking, you must deal with and handle people if you are to have power, influence and control over them. Here too, toward the same purpose but with a difference in manner, the whole secret of dealing with and handling people is in having the "guts" to do so!

8. Points worth special attention

1. You have more to lose by accommodating a trampler than by stopping him.

2. The only time it is easy to stop a trampler is the first time he tries.

3. The real trick to stopping tramplers lies in not bristling and in dishing out the "treatment" with no change of manner.

4. The beagle, whether male or female, has a contempt for kindness and graciousness and looks on it as a weakness.

5. Recognize the "drop something," "lose something," "helpless" and "infirmity" tricks of the beagles; if you have the maturity and worldliness needed to be a self power, you can tell the difference between the beagle tricks and the genuine.

6. Deal with beagles roughly; if ignoring them doesn't stop them, squelch them.

7. The only way to stop woodspussies is to frustrate them; you'll do it if you ignore their stench and wade right among them.

8. Have the "guts" to trample on tramplers and not worry about your job, to squelch beagles and not worry about offending them, and to ignore the stench of woodspussies and wade right through them.

9. Above all, remember always that the whole secret of dealing with and handling people is in having the "guts" to do so!

20

HOW TO HAVE POWER, INFLUENCE AND CONTROL OVER SUCCESS

What power, influence and control you have over your success is dependent on how much self power you achieve.

Success has an ever changing character; today's goals are only a stage in tomorrow's new ones.

Only when you find achievement exhilarating, or have a no-ceiling incentive for it, are you likely to go beyond the ordinary success levels.

Making your self power more complete will make your successes easier and quicker.

You are better equipped for success, and have a greater opportunity to achieve it, than any who have preceded you.

You have already been given everything you need for perfecting your self power and becoming a self power success. No self power has ever had more (to guide him) and very few ever had the benefit of as much. How great a self power you will be, and how much of success you will command, depends now on whether you look on this twentieth and last step as effecting your final completion as a self power or as but completing your casting as one.

1. How much or little of success you are satisfied to settle for controls how much you have

Many years ago I was counseled, "Success and perfection are alike and inseparable, and any time you accept anything as being either of them you are compromising with them and abandoning their challenge."

Half the world's wisdom and philosophy are wrapped in that one bit of counseling but it is mentioned here only to point up that it is you alone who determines your end point in anything, even in self power.

Success and perfection, in self power as in all things, is but a matter of degree. Your self power is never so perfect that it can't be further perfected nor so great a success that it can't be a greater success. Thus, though your knowledge and exercise of all the techniques and principles of self power can make you a self power, how perfect or successful a self power you eventually become depends on how much you put into furbishing, finishing and polishing that self power and your practice of it.

No one is going to drive you to any point of perfection. You can stop at any point, compromising there with perfection and success by accepting that degree of them as all you want or need. When you do stop though, remember it was you, not anything or anyone else, that stopped you. And then recognize that others who go on beyond you do so, not because they have more of something than you, but because they are not satisfied to settle for as little of perfection and success.

2. Never let your self power rest or take a holiday

Just as self power gives you power, influence and control over people, it also gives you power, influence and control over success itself for you measure your success by one thing only,—how fully you achieve your aims,—and this thing is determined alone by your self power and your skill in the exercise of it.

You engaged in your search for self power because you have certain aims (hopes, desires, goals) and because you recognize those aims as ones that can only be attained through self power. You looked to attainment of those aims as success and saw it as an end point to reach for, but now, as you go on toward those aims and near them, you will see attainment of them only as a stage of success. In fact, until you tire of the challenge of life and decide to be satisfied with what you are, where you are, and what you have, there will always be new and greater aims, each a new and greater success you want to reach for,—and thus there will always be new and greater needs for self power.

To have influence and control over success, you must have power over it, and you have that power over it when you control the thing that makes it possible, self power. In turn, how much control you have over self power depends on your consciousness of its importance.

If you are adequately conscious of how important your self power is to your success, you'll never let it rest or take a holiday. You'll be scrupulously attentive to its details and strive constantly for more and more perfection in how you wear it and exercise it. Most of all, no matter how much of it you have, you'll never be satisfied that you have it to the full; time and time again you will retravel the twenty steps to it as if you'd never explored them before and find more and more new in them every time.

3. If you don't already find power essential to your aims, or exhilarating, lift your eyes higher

In reviewing and discussing the twenty steps with one of the great self powers of industry a few years ago, I commented, "Every person wants to have power, influence and control over his or her own success; once you've given them all the tools and techniques and guides for achieving it though, what further can you give them to help them go beyond ordinary success and toward the ultimate?" His reply is one every person who strives for self power and success should read carefully and remember:

"Unless the person can be dealt with individually and personally and supplied with an incentive strong enough to pull him beyond the ordinary, there is nothing anyone can give him.

"Incentive is the only power that ever causes a person to go beyond ordinary achievement, whether it is in something he is making or doing, or whether it is in what he is or his success. If an individual has no incentive for doing more or better work than another, or for being a better person or greater success than another, you can't expect him to make an attempt at it and he won't.

"Any number of things, such as family, social, economic or other needs, or just plain pride, cause a person to push to certain work, success or personal levels, but those things all exert a compelling influence, pushing the person, and can only push him to a level that satisfies the need, never beyond it. Incentive, on the other hand, even when it's greed or vengeance, exerts a pulling influence and, when it's an incentive without a ceiling on it, it never stops pulling. The person who has such an incentive keeps going beyond and beyond until he dies,—or until some event destroys the incentive or takes it away.

"There is of course the rare individual who needs no incentive, who does more and better solely because he finds the doing exhilarating, like the rare race horse that runs faster and faster because he finds running exhilarating. That individual needs nothing to push him or pull him. In fact, though he enjoys rewards as acknowledgements of his accomplishments, he disdains and is offended by incentives.

'All of that leaves only one answer to the question: If a person finds power exhilarating or is one who has a no-ceiling incentive for it, he doesn't need anything more to help him go beyond and beyond as a self power. On the other hand, if a person isn't either of those, there's nothing he can be given,—except the advice to lift his eyes higher and higher and higher. It's not likely he'll follow that advice, but if he does, sooner or later his eyes will fasten on something he feels his life demands, something he must reach for and attain to make his life satisfying,—and when he does that he'll have what you want to give him and can't,—incentive."

4. Strength, as a firmness, is essential to your self power

You are one of the three types of power seekers that executive covered in his reply. If you are the third and last type he mentioned, then all that can be done here is to emphasize his advice by admonishing you to follow it. If you are either of the other two types, however, you need no advice and shouldn't take any from anyone,—you have a strength other people don't have and advice from those who are weaker than you would always be of a kind that would suggest you restrain rather than employ your strength.

To remind yourself of how important your strength is to you, go back to the very beginning of these twenty steps and review the four secrets of self power. All the steps subsequent to them have had one purpose, that of building for you the strength set forth. Without that strength you couldn't be a self power, for your power, influence and control over others is dependent on your strength in those things (striking instantly; making others want to bend to you; making them want to perform for you; and, making them want to enjoy a bond with you).

To further remind yourself of how important your strength is to you, go on to step two and review the power comparisons. Convince yourself once again that strength comes only from real power and that the only real power is self power, the power that comes from your self alone.

If your power is to have strength it can't have softness. However, the more of self power you gain, the more you will recognize that desirable strength results from firmness, not from hardness. Someone once likened a self power's strength to butter, pointing out that when you are too warm to people you are soft, when you are too cool toward people you are hard, but that when you are moderate you have the firmness that people appreciate.

5. Keep your sense and feel of self power fully alive

The five key factors in proper human intercourse (as set forth in step three) are your foundation stones for eminence and self power and you must keep them strong and alive at all times.

No self power can afford to forego constantly reminding himself of these factors. Whether you are a new self power or an experienced one, you need to review them regularly. Your remaining a self power depends first of all on your relations with others, not only with the strangers you encounter every day but also with those persons over whom you already have power, influence and control. Your foundation stones are the key to these relations and if you become inattentive to your foundation you topple your tower of power.

Through every day, in every encounter with people, and with strangers particularly, you must constantly be mindful of whether your self power is holding its vigor and making all people conscious of you. At the smallest sign that it may not be, go back to your foundation stones and coach yourself anew on the factors that gave you your first sense and feel of self power. Laxity in those more often than not is the cause of any waning of your self power. The experience of other self powers has shown that if you keep your sense and feel of self power fully alive there will be little likelihood of your being lax in the exercising of its techniques.

6. Taking time to make your mastery of the steps more complete will make your success quicker and more complete

Because the twenty steps have been presented for you here in a form that enables easy review and reminder, no summary of them is necessary. The box at the head of each chapter, along with the points enumerated for special attention at the close of each chapter, affords you a concise and complete summary in an easy reference manner and also simplifies for you any reference you need to make to material in the body of the chapters. To further simplify such reference for you, the key to what each subsection builds to has been used as the section heading in every instance.

The twenty steps that take you to self power and the power, influence and control you want over others, have been dealt with realistically and without dreamy theory or the pulling of any punches. The chapter headings themselves remind you forcefully of what these steps are but, because seeing them all at one glance helps to emphasize them and the order of their importance, the twenty steps are listed for you here:

1. Recognize what the secrets of self power are.
2. Evaluate self power and its uses.
3. Start your own self power generating.
4. Make all people conscious of you.
5. Make people want to know you.
6. Prime and warm up people.
7. Pull forth friendliness.
8. Listen aggressively.
9. Bag and pocket people.
10. Be on the offensive unoffendingly.
11. Strengthen your individuality.
12. Project individualism.
13. Make your thinking win.
14. Pull maximum cooperativeness.
15. Build the vigor of your self power.
16. Achieve and maintain maximum power effectiveness.
17. Rise with your power levels.
18. Win every power duel.
19. Promptly dispose of difficult people.
20. Have power, influence and control over your success.

The hardest lesson for most power seekers to learn is that they can't just choose some of the steps that strike their fancy and build self power from them. Similarly, that self power can't be built by being attentive to only such steps as they feel "meet a situation." Self power, and the success you want from it, is unattainable unless you give full (not partial) attentiveness to all steps at all times.

In mastering self power, you need to deal with the steps individually and in the order given, but once each is mastered it must be merged with those that have been mastered before it. Unless you follow that procedure and weld the steps into a solid unit your power, influence and control over others will always be weak and incomplete.

There are two things more that the experience of self powers has proved. One is that, in your first covering of the twenty steps, you missed the fine points that enable you to put a finish and polish on your self power. The other is that, as a new seeker of power, you have concentrated on the techniques and been inadequately attentive to the purposes and necessity of them.

No one likes to be sent back over ground already covered. Nevertheless, when you have lost something that is important to you, it is foolhardy to go on without first retraveling your steps to recover what has been lost. In this instance, your careful retraveling of the covered ground will enable you not only to gain what has been lost but will also save you valuable time in reaching the success that is all important to you.

7. Never ignore that you can be a self power only among those who accept you

The most ignored step of all the twenty is step seventeen, which deals with rising with your power levels. The power seeker, more than all other people, always sees that many persons do not fit into his level or environment but refuses to recognize that there are levels or environments into which he himself does not fit. As a consequence, he ignores the guides, admonishments and techniques of step seventeen and needlessly commits blunders.

There is no excuse for a self power ever suffering a defeat or setback. When he does suffer one, it is always because he has been lax and inattentive to one or more of those things from which his self power is forged. The most inexcusable of all setbacks though it is that which a self power suffers from not rising with his power levels. And it often is the hardest to overcome.

As put forth in the chapter dealing with step seventeen, the suggested technique is nothing more than a precaution one's own common sense should dictate. Any final word on self power must always emphasize that, for, no matter how great a self power you become, common sense should also tell you that you can't be a self power in any area where you mark yourself as not belonging.

8. You have every opportunity to be a greater power and success than any who have preceded you

No matter what your attitude toward life, purpose and people has been, the reading of *Twenty Steps to Power, Influence and Control Over People* has made changes in it, and it will change you. It probably hasn't inspired you and it hasn't intended to, but it has made you look at people and your dealing with them more realistically and practically than you ever have before.

Never before has the subject of self power been dealt with in printed form in the English language. Thus, here, for the first time, you have been given completely and concisely the whole of a subject that other self powers before you have had to gather in snatches by word of mouth or by the trial and error methods of hard (and sometimes sad and costly) experience. As remarked earlier, no one striving for power and success has ever had more than you have to begin with, and few ever have had as much. You have every opportunity to be greater than any of them.

9. Points worth special attention

1. The acceptance of anything as success or perfection is compromising with success and perfection and abandoning their challenge.

2. Your success is dependent on your self power; never let it rest or take a holiday.

3. Never be satisfied that you have self power to the full.

4. If you want to go beyond the ordinary, find a no-ceiling incentive and your success will take care of itself.

5. You can't be soft and be strong as a self power; firmness, not hardness, is a strength people respect and appreciate.

6. Maintaining awareness of the foundation stones of self power will keep your sense and feel of self power alive.

7. Self power, and the success you want from it, is unattainable unless you give full attentiveness to all twenty steps at all times.

8. Put special attention on rising with your levels; no setback is so inexcusable as the one that results from marking yourself as not belonging.

9. Dealing with people has been made realistic and practical for you for the first time; you are better equipped to achieve power and success than any who have ever attained either of them.